S0-ABB-409

GRADES K–2

A Guide *to the*

TEACHERS COLLEGE READING AND WRITING PROJECT

Classroom Libraries

Curated by

LUCY CALKINS ✦ MOLLY PICARDI
KATIE WEARS ✦ AND COLLEAGUES

Heinemann

DEDICATED TO TEACHERS™

Heinemann
361 Hanover Street
Portsmouth, NH 03801–3912
www.heinemann.com
Offices and agents throughout the world

© 2016 by Lucy Calkins

All rights reserved. No part of this book may be reproduced in any form or by any electronic or mechanical means, including information storage and retrieval systems, without permission in writing from the publisher, except by a reviewer, who may quote brief passages in a review.

The authors have dedicated a great deal of time and effort to writing the content of this book, and their written expression is protected by copyright law. We respectfully ask that you do not adapt, reuse, or copy anything on third-party (whether for-profit or not-for-profit) lesson-sharing websites. As always, we're happy to answer any questions you may have.

—**Heinemann Publishers**

"Dedicated to Teachers" is a trademark of Greenwood Publishing Group, Inc.

The authors and publisher wish to thank those who have generously given permission to reprint borrowed material:

Mouse Has Fun: Cat and Mouse. Text copyright © 2002 by Phyllis Root. Illustrations copyright © 2002 by James Croft. Reproduced by permission of the publisher, Candlewick Press.

Can You See the Eggs? By Jenny Giles. Copyright © 2013 HMH Supplemental Publishers. Used by permission of Cengage Australia.

Swimming with Mermaids, © 2014 Michele Dufresne. Reprinted courtesy of Pioneer Valley Books.

Ollie the Stomper, by Olivier Dunrea. Copyright © 2003 by Houghton Mifflin. Reprinted by permission of Houghton Mifflin Harcourt Publishing Company.

Puppy Trouble, © 2006 Michele Dufresne. Reprinted courtesy of Pioneer Valley Books.

From Stavetski, Barbara, I'M TOO TALL, part of the KING SCHOOL SERIES. Copyright © 2009 by Townsend Press.

In the Days of Dinosaurs: The Dinosaur Chase, by Hugh Price. Copyright © 2013 HMH Supplement Publishers. Used by permission of Cengage Australia.

From *Iris and Walter and the Field Trip,* by Elissa Haden Guest. Illustrated by Christine Davenier. Copyright © 2001. Reprinted by permission of Houghton Mifflin Harcourt Publishing Company.

Days with Frog and Toad, by Arnold Lobel. Text copyright © 1979 by Arnold Lobel. Used by permission of HarperCollins Publishers.

Library of Congress Cataloging-in-Publication Data is on file with the Library of Congress.

ISBN-13: 978-0-325-08974-4

Editors: Karen Kawaguchi and Tracy Wells
Production: Elizabeth Valway, David Stirling, and Abigail Heim
Cover and interior designs: Jenny Jensen Greenleaf
Photography: Peter Cunningham
Composition: Publishers' Design and Production Services, Inc.
Manufacturing: Steve Bernier

Printed in the United States of America on acid-free paper
23 22 21 20 19 B&B 5 6 7 8 9

Contents

Contributors
and
Consultants
from the Field

Teachers College Reading and Writing Project

The entire staff of the Teachers College Reading and Writing Project contributed to and supported the work on this vast curation project. Particular thanks go to:

Marissa Altamura, Project Coordinator

Carl Anderson, Staff Developer; speaker; author

Maggie Beattie Roberts, Lead Staff Developer; presenter; author and Units of Study for Teaching Writing series coauthor

Heather Burns, Staff Developer; former teacher and literacy coach

Lucy Calkins, Founding Director; Teachers College/Columbia University Robinson Professor of Children's Literature and Literacy Specialist Program co-director; leading literacy authority and keynote speaker; author or coauthor of numerous books, including the Units of Study for Teaching Reading/Writing series

Katie Clements, Staff Developer; Units of Study for Reading/Writing series author/coauthor

M. Colleen Cruz, Senior Lead Staff Developer; author; former teacher

Mary Ehrenworth, Deputy Director for Middle Schools; author; Units of Study for Teaching Reading/Writing series author/coauthor

Kimberly Fox, Staff Developer; former special education teacher; Units of Study series illustrator

Elizabeth Franco, Senior Research Associate; former teacher; Units of Study for Teaching Reading/Writing series author/coauthor/illustrator

Simone Fraser, Staff Developer; former upper grade elementary teacher

Shana Frazin, Staff Developer; Units of Study for Writing series coauthor

Brooke Geller, Senior Lead Staff Developer; Units of Study for Teaching Reading coauthor

Eric Hand, Staff Developer; former teacher

Kelly Boland Hohne, Writer in Residence, Senior Research Associate; Units of Study for Reading/Writing series author/coauthor

Norah Mallaney, Literacy Specialist (Grades 3–5); former teacher

Marjorie Martinelli, Senior Research Associate; co-director of Reading Rescue; "ChartChums" blogger; author and Units of Study for Teaching Reading/Writing series coauthor/illustrator

Michelle McGrath, Staff Developer; former teacher-researcher, mentor, and teacher

Heather Michael, Staff Developer (grades 6–8); Teachers College Curriculum and Teaching Doctoral program student; former teacher

Mary Ann Mustac, Executive Assistant

Mike Ochs, Staff Developer; Teachers College Literacy Specialist program; Units of Study for Teaching Reading/Writing series coauthor

Leah Bragin Page, Staff Developer; former general education and inclusion teacher and literacy coach

Molly Picardi, Staff Developer (Grades K–2); Teachers College Literacy Specialist program graduate student

Alissa Reicherter, Staff Developer; Units of Study for Teaching Reading series coauthor

Kate Roberts, Staff Developer; presenter; author and Units of Study for Teaching Writing series coauthor; former middle school teacher and literacy coach

Cynthia Satterlee, Staff Developer; former teacher

Emily Butler Smith, Senior Research Associate, Lead Staff Developer; Units of Study for Teaching Writing/Reading series coauthor

Kristin Smith, Staff Developer; Units of Study for Teaching Reading series coauthor; former teacher

Janet Steinberg, Research and Data Manager; Units of Study for Teaching Reading series coauthor; former literacy coach

Kathleen Tolan, Senior Deputy Director; Units of Study for Teaching Reading/Writing series author/coauthor

Katie Wears, Staff Developer; Units of Study for Teaching Reading series coauthor; former K–8 literacy coach

Pablo Wolfe, Staff Developer; former teacher

Children's Literature and Education/Literacy Experts

Richard Allington, Professor of Education, University of Tennessee; past president of IRA, NRC; editorial advisory board member for numerous scholarly education journals and publications; author

Alyson Beecher, "Kid Lit Frenzy" blogger

Kylene Beers, educational consultant; presenter; author

Lois Bridges, literacy publisher and editor, Scholastic; literacy specialist; former teacher and consultant

Katherine Bomer, educational consultant; teacher; author

Randy Bomer, literacy consultant; Professor, College of Education, University of Texas; author; TCRWP former co-director; past president of NCTE

David Booth, Professor Emeritus in Education, Coordinator of Elementary Programs at Ontario Institute for Studies in Education, University of Toronto; literacy consultant; speaker; author

Louise Cappizzo, "The Nonfiction Detectives" blogger

Betty Carter, Professor Emerita of Children's and Young Adult Literature, Texas Woman's University; former reading teacher and school librarian

Anna Gratz Cockerille, literacy consultant; "Two Writing Teachers" blogger and Heinemann blog editor; Units of Study in Teaching Writing coauthor; former TCRWP staff developer, Heinemann editor, and teacher

Kathy Collins, literacy consultant; presenter; author; former teacher

Smokey Daniels, literacy consultant; presenter; author; former teacher, teacher-educator, and editor

Diane DeFord, Professor, Language and Literacy Instruction and Teacher Education, University of Southern Carolina; author

Ralph Fletcher, literacy consultant; presenter; author

Judy Freeman, children's literature consultant and book reviewer; speaker; author

Don Futterman, Executive Director, Israel Center for Educational Innovation

Emily Gasoi, Senior Consultant, Artful Education; former teacher

Carrie Gelson, "There's a Book for That" blogger

Anne Goudvis, staff developer, Public Education and Business Coalition; literacy consultant; author; former teacher

Stephanie Harvey, literacy consultant; presenter; author; former Public Education and Business Coalition staff developer; former teacher

Georgia Heard, presenter; poet; author; former TCRWP senior staff developer

Ellin Keene, literacy consultant; presenter; author; former teacher, professor, and staff developer at the Public Education and Business Coalition

Penny Kittle, literacy consultant; presenter; author; teacher

Lester Laminack, Professor Emeritus, Western Carolina University; literacy and children's literature consultant; presenter; author

Alexandra Marron, former TCRWP senior research associate, staff developer, writer-in-residence; Units of Study for Teaching Reading/Writing series author/coauthor

Liz Rosado-McGrath, national content specialist, Heinemann Publishing; former teacher, EL specialist

Donalyn Miller, Grades 4–6 teacher; presenter; author

Heidi Mills, Professor, Department of Instruction and Teacher Education, University of South Carolina; founding member, Center for Inquiry; literacy consultant; presenter; author

Kate Montgomery, international literacy consultant; author; former editor and TCRWP lead researcher and teacher

Elizabeth Moore, literacy coach and consultant; "Two Writing Teachers" blogger; Units of Study in Reading/Teaching Writing series coauthor; former teacher and TCRWP staff developer

Kristine Mraz, educational consultant; author; teacher; "ChartChums" blogger; former TCRWP staff developer

The Nerdy Book Club online blog community

Cathy Potter, "The Nonfiction Detectives" blogger

Jen Serravallo, literacy consultant; presenter; author; former TCRWP staff developer and teacher

Anita Silvey, former editor-in-chief of *The Horn Book Magazine*; author

Pam Smith, national content specialist, Heinemann Publishing; educational consultant; former principal and teacher

Katherine Sokolowski, "Nerdy Book Club" and "Read, Write, Reflect" blogger

Elizabeth Sulzby, Professor of Education, University of Michigan; emergent literacy author and expert

Jim Trelease, author; former presenter

Gita Varadarajan, literacy coach and consultant

Jennifer Vincent, "Teach Mentor Texts" blogger

Judy Wallis, staff development and literacy consultant; author; former teacher, literacy coach, and university instructor

Joe Yukish, educational consultant; presenter; author; former TCRWP Director, Senior Primary Reading Adviser, and Reading Recovery professor

Teachers and Librarians

Alyssa Agoston, Grade 1 teacher, Elms Elementary School, Jackson, NJ

Rebecca Anderson, media center clerk, Las Virgenes Unified School District, Calabasas, CA

Christa Anderson, literacy leader, Middleton-Cross Plains Area School District, Middleton, WI

Barbara Andrews, literacy specialist, Las Virgenes Unified School District, Calabasas, CA

Lisa Badalamenti, reading specialist, NYC Board of Education, New York, NY

Lindsay Barna, literacy content area specialist and coach, Piscataway Township Schools, Piscataway, NJ

Jennifer Barnes, Grades K–1 teacher, Center for Inquiry, Richland County School District Two, Columbia, SC

Amanda Blake, Grades 4–5 teacher, Center for Inquiry, Richland County School District Two, Columbia, SC

Karan Bliske, teacher, Marshall Public Schools, Marshall, WI

Sarah Boland, special education teacher, George G. White Middle School, Hillsdale, NJ

Susan Bolte, Grades K–1 teacher, Center for Inquiry, Richland County School District Two, Columbia, SC

Kristen Bourn, teacher, ISG American School of Jubail, Saudi Arabia

Nancy Boyd, librarian, East Hills School, Roslyn, NY

Nancy Bradley, instructional coach, Exley Elementary School, Katy, TX

Tameka Breland, Grades 4–5 teacher, Center for Inquiry, Richland County School District Two, Columbia, SC

Kristen Brennan, instructional coach, Bonnie Holland Elementary School, Katy, TX

Patricia Bryan, Grade 6 teacher, English East Side Community School, New York, NY

Sonja Cherry-Paul, teacher, Farragut Middle School, Hastings-on-Hudson, NY; professional development consultant; author

Michele Ciconte, Grade 2 teacher, Tatnall School, Wilmington, DE

Jaleelah Cooke, principal, and the entire staff at PS 369, Brooklyn, NY

Marija Crosson, Grade 4 teacher, Mastery Charter Schools, Philadelphia, PA

Elizabeth Culkin, principal, PS 176, New York, NY

Deb Dagitz, library media specialist, Elm Lawn Elementary School, Middleton, WI

Jenni Darby-Lanker, teacher, Gresham-Barlow School District, Portland, OR

Nicole Dixon, Grade 7 ELA teacher, Eastside Community School, New York, NY

Tomi Dodson, Grade 2 teacher, Stephens Elementary School, Houston, TX

Justin Dolci, ELA teacher, Jefferson County Public Schools, Louisville, KY

Kitty Donohoe, teacher, Santa Monica, CA

Brenna Dorgan, Grade 4 teacher, Stephens Elementary School, Houston, TX

Kathy Doyle, retired teacher; former teacher-pilot for TCRWP and Units of Study series

Dina Ercolano, principal, PS 158, New York, NY

Sonhando Estwick, principal, Tompkins Square Middle School, New York, NY

Rebecca Fagin, principal, PS 29, New York, NY

Stacey Fell, teacher, Tompkins Square Middle School, New York, NY; Units of Study for Teaching Writing series coauthor

Michelle Fiorini, teacher, Benjamin Middle School, West Chicago, IL

Lauren Fontana, principal, PS 6, New York, NY

Gina Fontana, curriculum specialist and literacy coach, LCC Day School, St. Petersburg, FL

Brandon Foote, Grades 2–3 teacher, Center for Inquiry, Richland County School District Two, Columbia, SC

Laurie Foote, teacher, North Clackamas School District, Milwaukie, OR

Ben Frazell, instructional coach, Inspired Teaching Public Charter School, Washington, DC

Tracey Fritch, Grade 6 ELA teacher, Springton Lake Middle School, Media, PA

Liza Garza, bilingual programs instructional officer, Katy Independent School District, Katy, TX

Mary Catherine Gregorio, Grade 4 teacher, Millstone River School, Plainsboro, NJ

Matt Halpern, K–5 literacy strategist, Regional School Unit 5, Freeport, ME

Stephanie Hardinger, Grades 4–5 lead teacher, East Palo Alto Charter School, Aspire Public Schools, Palo Alto, CA

Jade Hargrave, Grade 1 teacher, Nathaniel Morton Elementary, Plymouth, MA

Marie Hartney, Middle School ELA teacher, LCC Day School, St. Petersburg, FL

Chris Hass, Grades 2–3 teacher, Center for Inquiry, Richland County School District Two, Columbia, SC

Heathcote Elementary School teachers, Scarsdale, NY

Carrie Hepburn, elementary ELA content leader, Francis Howell School District, Saint Charles, MO

Allison Hepfer, teacher, Bethlehem Central School District, Glenmont, NY

Erin Hermann, literacy specialist/coach, Colchester Elementary School, Colchester, CT

Kaitlyn Holloway, Grade 1 teacher, Elms Elementary School, Jackson, NJ

Stephanie Jackson, teacher, Twin Falls School District, Idaho Falls, ID

Alyna Jacobs, principal, South Mountain Elementary School, South Orange, NJ

Dana Johansen, Grade 5 English teacher, Greenwich Academy, Greenwich, CT; presenter; author

Juliana Johnson, K–3 curriculum and instruction teacher resource specialist, West Windsor-Plainsboro Regional School District; West Windsor, NJ

Scott Johnson, Grades 4–5 teacher, Center for Inquiry, Richland County School District Two; Columbia, SC

Alicia Felts Jones, instructional content facilitator, Union County Public Schools, Monroe, NC

Jasmine Junsay, teacher, PS 29, New York, NY

Renee Keeler, teacher, grade 3, Lee Elementary School, Los Alamitos, CA

Melissa Klosterman, Grades K–1 teacher, Center for Inquiry, Richland County School District Two, Columbia, SC

Sandy Kope, teacher, grade 1, Canyon Creek Elementary, Bothell, WA

Peter Kornicker, librarian; PS 161, New York, NY

Kristen Kowalick, Kindergarten teacher, John Hancock Demonstration Elementary School, Philadelphia, PA

Stephanie Kramer, teacher, Menahga Public Schools, Menahga, MN

Lisa Lane, assistant principal, Jackson School District, Jackson, NJ

Jennifer Latimer, school media specialist, Clinton Elementary School, Maplewood, NJ

Michael Lewis, Grade 5 teacher, Deer Hill School, Cohasset, MA; Apple Distinguished Educator; author

Ginny Lockwood, principal, Mamaroneck Avenue School, Mamaroneck, NY

Deborah Longo, preK site coordinator, Targee Street Pre-K Center, New York, NY

Allison Lucchesi, Grade 4 teacher, E.M. Baker School, Great Neck, NY

Adam Marcus, librarian, PS 32K, New York, NY

Maria Maroni, teacher, Stow-Munroe Falls Schools, Stow-Munroe, OH

Cindy Marten, superintendent, San Diego Unified School District; literacy specialist; author

Carole Mashamesh, Grade 7 humanities teacher, Tompkins Square Middle School, New York, NY

Gianna Matchniff, Grade 1 teacher, Heron Heights Elementary School, Parkland, FL

Casey Maxwell, Kindergarten teacher, PS 446, New York, NY

Lynne McCune, literacy specialist, Colchester Public Schools, Colchester, CT

Monica McDearmon, Grade 6 teacher, Chickahominy Middle School, Mechanicsville, VA

Medea McEvoy, principal, PS 267, New York, NY

Jenna McMahon, Grades 1–2 teacher, Kiel School, Kinnelon, NJ

Jessie Miller, ELA and SS curriculum coordinator, Katy Independent School District, Katy, TX

Kate Mills, teacher, grade 4, Knollwood Elementary School, Fair Haven, NJ

Stacey Moore, curriculum coach, Van Buren School District, Van Buren, AR

Bridget Mullett, teacher, Pitner Elementary School, Acworth, GA

Tim O'Keefe, Grades 2–3 teacher, Center for Inquiry, Richland County School District Two, Columbia, SC

Patricia O'Rourke, Grade 2 teacher, ReNEW Schools Charter Management Organization, New Orleans, LA

Jill Osmerg, curriculum support teacher, Woodland Elementary School, Sandy Springs, GA

Tiffany Palmtier, Grades K–1 teacher, Center for Inquiry, Richland County School District Two, Columbia, SC

Danielle Parella, Grade 1 teacher, Elms Elementary School, Jackson, NJ

Meredith-Leigh Pleasants, instructional coach, ReNEW Schools Charter Management Organization, New Orleans, LA

Jennifer Rodman Priddy, Grade 4 teacher, St. Paul's School, Brooklandville, MD

PS 6 teachers, New York, NY

PS 29 teachers, New York, NY

PS 59 teachers, New York, NY

PS 158 teachers, New York, NY

PS 176 teachers, New York, NY

PS 267 teachers, New York, NY

Jeny Randall, teacher, language arts/intermediate and upper science, Saratoga Independent School, Saratoga Springs, NY

Lisa Raney, Grade 2 teacher, Elms Elementary School, Jackson, NJ

Miriam Regan, Kindergarten teacher, Schaumburg Elementary ReNEW Charter School, New Orleans, LA

Rachel Reilly, Grade 2 teacher, Sharon Elementary School, Robbinsville, NJ

Brooke Rennie, Grade 8 ELA teacher, The Learning Community Charter School, Central Falls, RI

Kelli Rich, teacher, Mason City Schools, Mason City, OH

Marni Rogers, literacy coach, Gwinnett County Public Schools, Gwinnett, GA

Laura Salopek, reading teacher, Deforest Middle School, Deforest, WI

Donna Santman, academic director, Harlem Village Academies, New York, NY; educational consultant; author; former TCRWP staff developer

Adele Schroeder, principal, PS 59, New York, NY

Denise Schweikart, literacy coach, Greenwood School District 50, Greenwood, SC

Michele Shipman, assistant principal, Van Buren School District, Van Buren, AR

Gillian Shotwell, instructional coach, PS 249, New York, NY

Josephine Sinagra, teacher, PS 139, New York, NY

Valerie Stanley, teacher, Lyon County School District, Yerington, NV

Elisabeth Stephens and her class, Grade 5 teacher, PS 29, New York, NY

Kim Stieber-White, library media specialist, Glacier Creek Middle School, Cross Plains, WI

Maria R. Stile, principal, Heathcote Elementary School, Scarsdale, NY

Kate Sweeney, library media specialist, J. O. Wilson Elementary School, Washington, DC

Andrea Swenson, librarian, Eastside Middle School, New York, NY

Melanie Swider, literacy coach, Simsbury Schools, Simsbury, CT

Lori Talish, teacher/librarian, PS 59, New York, NY

Robyn Thomas, Grades PreK–2 lead learning coach, Mason City Schools, Mason City, OH

Tompkins Square Middle School teachers, New York, NY

Caryn Alexander Tsagalis, Grade 1 teacher, Cherokee Elementary School, Lake Forest, IL

Rachel Venegas, Kindergarten teacher, E.M. Baker School, Great Neck, NY

Aimee Volk, Grade 3 teacher, Kreamer Street Elementary School, Patchogue, NY

Kristen Robbins Warren, Grades 7–8 ELA teacher, NYC Department of Education; "A Kind of a Library" blogger

Jenny Weber, teacher, Horace Mann Elementary School, Washington, DC

Nora Wentworth, teacher, Akili Academy, New Orleans, LA

Emily Whitecotton, Grades 4–5 teacher, Center for Inquiry, Richland County School District Two, Columbia, SC

Deb Zaffiro, instructional coach, Greenfield Public Schools, Greenfield, WI

Teachers College, Columbia University

Alicia Andres-Arroyo, graduate student

Rebecca Bellingham, Professor of Education

Alice Day Brown, graduate student

Ellen Ellis, Professor of Education

Karen Finnerty, graduate student

Nicole Fristachi, Administrative Assistant

Maria Paula Ghiso, Assistant Professor of Literacy Education

Ed Hodson, graduate student

Noel Imbriale, graduate student

Maria Souto Manning, Associate Professor of Early Childhood Education

Elizabeth Massi, graduate student

Vincent Phram, graduate student

Laura Schwartz, graduate student

Marjorie Siegel, Professor of Education

Jennifer Snyder, graduate student

Brittania Surles, graduate student

Publishers, Bookstores, Book Clubs, and Suppliers

ABDO Publishing

Abrams Books

Albert Whitman & Company

American Girl Publishing

Arbordale Publishing

Arte Publico Press

Bank Street Bookstore, NYC

Barefoot Books

Barron's Educational Series

Bearport Publishing

Bellwether Media

Blueberry Hill Books

Bookmasters

Books of Wonder

Booksource: Special thanks to Michelle Abeln, Cheryl Dickemper, Diona Graves, and
    Brandi Ivester, collection development specialists

Brilliance Publishing (Amazon.com)

Candlewick Press

Capstone Publishing

Charlesbridge Publishing

Chronicle Books

Cinco Puntos Press

Crabtree Publishing

Creston Books

Cricket Books

Dawn Publications

DK Eyewitness Books (Penguin Random House)

Eerdmans

Enslow Publishers

Firefly Books

Flying Start Books

Hachette Book Group

Hameray Publishing

HarperCollins Children's Books

HarperCollins

Heinemann

Holiday House Books

Houghton Mifflin Harcourt

House of Anansi Press (Groundwood)

Hyperion Books

Independent Publishers Group

Kaeden Books

Kids Can Press

Kirkus Review

Ko Kids Books

Lee & Low Books

Lerner Publishing Group

Macmillan Publishers

Mary Ruth Books

McSweeney's Quarterly & Books

Microcosm Publishing

Midpoint Publishing

Mighty Media Press

Milkweed Editions

National Geographic Kids

National Geographic Partners

National Geographic Society

Okapi Educational Publishing

Orca Book Publishers

Owlkids Books

PeachTree Publishers

Penguin Books

Penguin Random House

Perseus Books Group

Pioneer Valley Books

Publisher's Group Worldwide

Random House Kids

Reading Reading Books

Richard C. Owen Publishers

RiverStream Publishing

Rosen Publishing

Saddleback Educational Publishing

Saunders Book Company

Scholastic

Seedling Resources (Continental Press)

Shelter Publications

Silver Dolphin Books

Simon & Schuster

Sourcebooks

Stenhouse Publishers

Sterling Publishing

Sundance Publishing

Tanglewood Press

Teacher Created Materials

Toon Books

Top Shelf Productions

Townsend Press

Trinity University Press

Web of Life Children's Books

Workman Publishing

A Note of Special Thanks

We are grateful to everyone who offered time or expertise to the Classroom Libraries project, but we would like to extend special thanks to the following individuals whose contributions were particularly crucial to its success: Alicia Andres-Arroyo, David Booth, Heather Burns, Kathy Doyle, Karen Finnerty, Abby Heim, Noel Imbriale, Jasmine Junsay, Penny Kittle, Michael Lewis, Heidi Mills, Tim O'Keefe, Leah Bragin Page, Vincent Phram, Laura Schwartz, Jennifer Snyder, Teachers of NYC PS 6, Teachers of NYC PS 158, Teachers of Heathcote Elementary School, Julia Tolan, Pablo Wolfe, and Joe Yukish.

Chapter 1

Letter to Teachers

Dear Teachers,

For the Teachers College Reading and Writing Project (TCRWP), this effort to create Classroom Libraries has been an all-important mission: to build state-of-the-art Classroom Libraries filled with awe-inspiring, spine-tingling, mind-bending books that deeply engage children, strengthen reading and thinking skills, and inspire kids to become lifelong readers.

As I write this letter, I'm trying to picture who you are, where you are. I like to think that this *Guide* for the Teachers College Reading and Writing Project Classroom Libraries lies on top of a giant box filled to the brim with the library you have ordered, or perhaps one or more shelves to begin or continue growing your Classroom Library, and that you'll think of this *Guide* as an introduction to that library.

The shelves in the boxes you are opening were curated by the entire staff of the Teachers College Reading and Writing Project. We combined our ideas with those of other reading and literature experts, teachers, librarians, and children, to thoughtfully collect, examine, and select books—books that will make a difference in the lives of children as readers and learners.

The TCRWP Classroom Libraries were created in a way that is worlds apart from how most other libraries are created. The Classroom Libraries Project began with our scouring the world to find the best literacy coaches, top experts in teaching reading and writing, renowned librarians, and mentor teachers who love books. Then we asked those experts to join our cause. We reached out to respected pros on children's literature, soliciting book recommendations from everyone. We got recommendations from people you know—Katherine and Randy Bomer, David Booth, Lois Bridges, Ralph Fletcher, Maria Paula Ghiso, Stephanie Harvey, Lester Laminack, Mariana Souto Manning, Heidi Mills, Betty Carter, Anita Silvey, people from the Nerdy Book Club, all of our own staff and from hundreds of literacy coaches, authors, and teachers. We explained to each of the people that we approached that for TCRWP, this is a mission of love. All of TCRWP's profits from this will be plowed back into an ongoing effort to provide kids with the best possible classroom libraries.

Eventually we had lists of recommendations from hundreds of experts. We then get copies of the more than 22,000-plus books that had been recommended. All of us at TCRWP worked tirelessly for half a year in a gigantic basement—inventorying, leveling, reviewing, curating shelves. For every book that we selected, there were scores of others that we set aside.

This, then, is what sets this work apart from other classroom libraries made by lone teachers, or created by a few people at a book distributor or a publisher (which are often limited to the books that publisher puts out or has bought the rights to).

Also, these Classroom Libraries are not the good-for-you, cod-liver-oil sort of libraries. Time-honored classics are included here, but many books are the cutting-edge, imaginative titles that kids today will love—the Dory Fantasmagory, Discover Our World, Quack the Duck, Mercy Watson, and Princess in Black series, and the *Diva and Flea* kinds of books. We carefully chose books based on kids' interests and on the richness of the books, books that can be mined again and again. We also looked for quality of writing and content, and for a diverse range of genres, topics, and author styles that support reading skills up the ladder.

Just for a moment, think about the astronomical amounts of money this nation has spent over the last decade to diagnose and "cure" reading deficiencies. Think of the billions of dollars' worth of tests that are constantly developed to ferret out kids' deficits. Think of how readers (and teachers) have been blamed and shamed in the public square. Think of the resources poured into developing worksheets and software programs that make kids detest reading. None of that has turned kids into readers. None of that has done the job that Mrs. Wishy-Washy and Mercy Watson have done!

My colleagues and I think of the TCRWP Classroom Libraries as a statement to politicians and policy makers, educational leaders, and the rest. *This* is what kids need to become readers. Not those tests, not those programs, not those skills and drills, but amazing, thrilling *books*.

We laugh at memories of our early efforts to supply our own classrooms with libraries. Most of us remember walking into a bare room in August—and staring at those near-empty bookshelves. We remember that frantic feeling when we had to fill our shelves with *something*. Molly raced around a book warehouse sale, piling out-of-date books into bags—$20 per bag. Norah Mallaney (one of the Grades 3–5 library curators) went to a public library, filling a milk crate with *any* book that seemed remotely within reach for her kids. Shana Frazin (also a 3–5 curator) dug out musty copies of *National Geographic* magazines to substitute for books. Of course, this effort to move heaven and earth to provide kids with books has become part of what it means to be a teacher.

But the truth is that scooping any ol' book from warehouse shelves is no way to provision a classroom with the one single resource that will make the biggest difference in children's lives as learners. Think of it this way. Would you dream of teaching *math* by scooping up any ol' picked-over math books from rummage sales and warehouse closings? Not a chance. Instead, you'd bring together the professionals who love math and know it deeply. You'd ask them to help you research approaches to math. You'd search high and low for books that could help you teach math in clear, compelling, research-based ways. Teaching literacy deserves at least as much!

Think about the number of kids who hate to read. A study by the American Library Association showed that when asked, the day before graduating from high school, "Will you voluntarily pick up a book after graduation?" 85% of America's kids said, "No way." And that is 85% of the kids who stayed in school long enough to graduate—another huge group dropped out long before graduation!

If you and I had to select all our books from leftover remnants, wouldn't we also be turned off from reading? Considering what we've all been through as teachers, we're flabbergasted there hasn't been more talk and more work over the past few decades around developing high-quality classroom libraries. We think the mission of the TCRWP Classroom Library Project to put heart-stopping, gut-wrenching, glorious books into the hands of kids is critical. We believe that once these libraries reach children's hands, nothing on earth can *keep* them from reading.

Although you and your school system have spent a fair sum on these collections, even the complete libraries are designed as "starter" shelves. You will need more books. But the good news is that you and your kids will have the momentum and the energy—and the passion to get those books. Your kids will be willing to write petitions, make and sell bead necklaces and bookmarks, help wrap books at a local bookstore—*anything* to continue developing their library.

Because these Classroom Libraries have been carefully structured, we expect that as you secure more books, you'll fill out and extend the existing structure. You and your kids might find other books for a nonfiction topic-based subcategory like "All in a Day's Work." You may suggest that a new category—perhaps "Dangerous Animals"—be added to your nonfiction library. Your kids might announce that the shelf labeled "If you liked *Those Darn Squirrels*, you will like . . ." needs new additions. (See Chapter 3: "Setting Up, Introducing, and Managing Your Classroom Library," for information about the tools for the complete TCRWP Classroom Libraries, including book bin labels.)

As you prepare to set up your new Classroom Library, we hope you'll consult this *Guide* to help you and your students get oriented, as well as provide guidance on organizing and making the best use of your new library. In this *Guide*, you'll find discussions on topics including:

■ the research base for the development of the TCRWP Classroom Libraries

■ how to set up, introduce, and manage your library

- the content of shelves and how books were selected

- assessment, leveling of books, and matching books to readers

- overviews of teaching methods for read-alouds, shared reading, independent reading, partner reading, and conferring.

Richard Allington, past president of the International Reading Association, has written and spoken often about the three things that readers need to flourish: access to books they find fascinating, protected time to read, and expert instruction. We hope these libraries will provide you and your students with the first of these, will inspire you to protect the second, and allow you to focus on the third.

—Lucy Calkins

Chapter 2

Research Base for the TCRWP Classroom Libraries

Keeping students engaged in reading and learning might make it possible to overcome insuperable barriers to academic success.

(Brozo, Shiel, and Topping 2011)

The books in this library represent a big investment. People may ask, "How does one know if it's worth it—investing in books, like this? What's the research base for this decision?"

The truth is that the research base is so deep, so thorough, and so long-standing that anyone who works in reading knows that investing in books is a wise choice. If the goal is to support growth in reading, there are few decisions that will have more payoff than the decision to give students access to high-quality and high-interest fiction and nonfiction.

A recent study that has been highly influential is a global study instigated by the International Literacy Association. The ILA tasked a team of researchers to investigate the relationship between students' reading engagement and their academic success, as measured by the Programme for International Student Assessment (PISA) exam and also by grade point averages. The PISA exam measures an extremely high level of literacy—the kind of higher-order thinking and critical, analytical reading that we most want all our students to be skilled at.

This ILA study found that "attitude toward reading, frequency of leisure reading, and diversity of reading materials" were critical variables in not just reading achievement but academic achievement as measured by grade point averages (Brozo, Shiel, and Topping 2011, 311).

What was fascinating about this study is how reading for pleasure mitigated benefits and disadvantages of income. "Youth from the lowest socioeconomic

status (SES) who were highly engaged readers performed as well on the assessments as highly engaged youth from the middle SES group" (308). In fact, using regression analysis, the ILA study suggests that "keeping students engaged in reading and learning might make it possible for them to overcome what might otherwise be insuperable barriers to academic success" (308).

Creating opportunities for students to become engaged readers, it turns out, is a great tool of social justice. The sad truth is that many kids are growing up in this country with little or no access to books in their communities. In concentrated-poverty communities, the situation is especially dire. A recent study by Susan Neuman and Naomi Moland found that in Anacostia, a low-income neighborhood in Washington, D.C., not a single preschool-level book was available for sale, and stores in that neighborhood carried only five books for children in grades K–12—only one age-appropriate book for every 830 kids; that in sharp contrast to middle-income communities, where Neuman found in a 2001 study that there were 13 books available for each and every child in one middle-income Philadelphia neighborhood. With "book deserts" in many communities in this nation, it becomes even more urgent to give kids access to a plentiful supply of high-quality and high-interest books to support their reading lives.

Guthrie and Wigfield (2000) reinforce the significance of students reading fiction and nonfiction for pleasure, showing that the amount of knowledge that students gain from this kind of reading has a tremendous effect on all their academic achievement. Their study demonstrated that "as students become engaged readers, they provide themselves with self-generated learning opportunities that are equivalent to several years of education" (404). Engagement in reading, according to Guthrie and Wigfield, "may substantially compensate for low family income and poor educational background" (404). It makes sense. The more kids read, the more they know. The more they know, the more background knowledge they bring to their studies. The more they engage in content studies, the more they want to extend their reading.

Understanding the tremendous impact that reading engagement has on academic success leads to the question of how to develop children's reading skills and improve their engagement.

First, the research shows that children need enormous amounts of time for reading. Success in reading is directly related to the amount of time a person spends reading. Krashen points out that 93% of the tests on reading comprehension that collect data on volume of reading show that kids who are given more time to read do better (2004). Guthrie and Humenick found that reading volume predicted reading comprehension, and that dramatic increases in reading volume are important for thoughtful literacy proficiencies (2004). The NAEP Reading Report Card for the Nation (U.S. Department of Education 1999) showed that, at every level, reading more pages at home and at school was associated with higher reading scores.

The research also shows that children also need access to books that they can read with high levels of accuracy, fluency, and comprehension. Too often, only the students who can read well are given lots of opportunities in school for high-success reading, and as a result they flourish. Kids who can't read well come to school, ready for the promise of an education, and they're given impenetrable texts. Many studies support the need to provide children with books that are matched to them. Ehri et al. (2007) studied a specific tutoring program that was designed to support struggling first-grade English language learners, and after tracking the daily oral reading accuracy of the students, found that "the reading achievement of students who received . . . tutoring appeared to be explained primarily by one aspect of their tutoring experience—reading texts at a high level of accuracy, between 98% and 100%" (441). Swanson's (1999) meta-analysis of 180 intervention studies showed that for learning-disabled students, one of the three conditions that allow for achievement is that the difficulty level of the task must be controlled enough that the learner can be successful. Reading texts that are accessible is nowhere more important than for children who are beginning readers or who struggle.

Of course, the books that children read need to be varied, and to include both nonfiction and fiction. Research suggests that until recently, most students have had insufficient access to informational texts. One study of first-grade classrooms found that, on average, informational text constituted less than 10% of classroom libraries, and was supported by only 3% of materials displayed on walls and other surfaces in classrooms (Duke 2000). This study also showed that first-grade classrooms studied informational texts for only an average of 3.6 minutes a day. Lower-income children logged just 1.9 minutes a day of exposure to informational texts. A study by Goodwin and Miller (2012) supports the need for providing young readers with more information texts, suggesting that the average child in the U.S. currently spends just four minutes a day reading nonfiction. These libraries will change that data in important ways!

> *Increased exposure to information texts at an early age will help prepare students for the challenges of the nonfiction content they'll be reading in coming years.*

One reason it is critical for students to increase the time they spend reading nonfiction is that the strength of a student's general knowledge has a close relationship to the student's ability to comprehend complex nonfiction texts. Students who read a great deal of nonfiction gain knowledge about the world as well as about vocabulary. Research shows that even kindergarten-aged children can learn content and new language structures from exposure to informational texts (Duke and Bennett-Armistead 2003). In addition, the same researchers show that including more informational text in the classroom also has potential benefits. In a study of first-grade children with limited letter-sound knowledge, those in classrooms with more informational text had higher reading comprehension and writing levels by the end of the year than similar children in other classrooms. Reading nonfiction texts aloud in primary classrooms was also found to be beneficial. A study by Linda Kraemer and her colleagues (2012) concluded that first-grade children who were read information

texts three times a week for four weeks demonstrated an increased ability to comprehend nonfiction texts in comparison to their peers. The study suggests that increased exposure to information texts at an early age will help prepare students for the challenges of the nonfiction content they'll be reading in coming years.

Read-aloud is essential to teaching reading. There is far more to a powerful read-aloud than simply reading the text. Beck and McKeown remind us that "although reading a story to children is not a difficult task for a literate adult, taking advantage of the read-aloud experience to develop children's literacy is complex and demanding" (2001, 19). For the read-aloud to help students develop deep comprehension skills, it is important that the read-aloud provide teachers with an occasion for modeling think-alouds, and prompting for and then extending rich conversation. Research from Teale and Martinez (1996) suggests that there is something powerful that comes from the rich analytic talk that occurs when children are given the chance to reflect on a story. This kind of read-aloud, often referred to as interactive read-aloud, supports children as readers and thinkers.

Read-alouds are also a powerful method to teach vocabulary. We know from Hart and Risley (2003) that upon entering kindergarten, children from economically privileged homes have heard an estimated 30 million more words than children from economically disadvantaged homes. One of the ways to bridge this gap is through read-aloud. Research tells us that explicit instruction of sophisticated vocabulary in read-aloud texts, along with extended interaction with these words across the day, has a positive effect on children's overall vocabulary (Zipoli, Coyne, and McCoach 2010).

For young children, a read-aloud is also a sneak peek into what reading can be. Rasinski (2005) describes read-aloud being critical to fluency instruction because it provides an essential model for how reading should sound. Research also shows that reading aloud fosters positive attitudes toward reading in young children (Kotaman 2008), creates engagement in text (Sipe 2002), supports the development of oral language (Isabell et al. 2004), and strengthens comprehension (Kraemer et al. 2012; Trelease 2006). Of course, it also benefits children to hear a variety of texts across genres (Yopp and Yopp 2006; Kraemer et al. 2012). The fact is, as we read, we transmit more than just the story. We also model a mood, a stance, an engagement, and a fluency that bring out not just the meaning, but the feeling of the texts and how they go—features that, once children internalize them, make their independent engagement with their own texts far more effective.

When classroom libraries offer not only a wide range of books but also invitations for readers to choose from among those books, this leads to increased reading motivation. As Richard Allington puts it, "students read more, understand more, and are more likely to continue reading when they have the opportunity to choose what they read" (2012a, 10). Allington points to a meta-analysis by Guthrie and Humenick, which found that the two most powerful factors for increasing reading motivation and comprehension were (1) student access to many books and (2) personal choice of what to read (Allington 2012; Guthrie and Humenick 2004). Another recent study has shown that children's favorite books are ultimately the ones they choose on their own. These kids (ages six to seventeen) tend to finish reading these books through to the end (Scholastic Inc. and YouGov 2014).

Giving students the opportunity to learn to choose wisely from a wide variety of books inside of the classroom also helps them to choose appropriate texts outside of the classroom. This is a skill that Allington and his colleagues show "dramatically increases the likelihood that they will read outside of school" (Allington 2012a; Ivey and Broaddus 2001). Investing in books for children, then, is an investment in their growth during their tenure in school and beyond.

When you look at the books included in these classroom libraries, you'll see a strong emphasis on engaging titles. Teaching these readers strategies isn't going to be effective unless they actually choose to read. As the National Reading Panel puts it, "the importance of reading as an avenue to improved reading has been stressed by theorists, researchers, and practitioners alike, no matter what their perspectives. There are few ideas more widely accepted than that reading is learned through reading" (2000).

REFERENCES

Allington, R. 2012a. "Every Child, Every Day." *Educational Leadership* 69: 6, 10–15.
———. 2012b. *What Really Matters for Struggling Readers: Designing Research-Based Programs* (3rd ed.). Boston: Allyn and Bacon.
Beck, I. L., and M. G. McKeown. Sept. 2001. "Text Talk: Capturing the Benefits of Read-Aloud Experiences for Young Children." *The Reading Teacher* 55: 1, 10–20.
———. Jan. 2007. "Increasing Young Low-Income Children's Oral Vocabulary Repertoires through Rich and Focused Instruction." *The Elementary School Journal* 107: 3, 251–71.
Brozo, W. G. 2002. *To Be a Boy, to Be a Reader: Engaging Teen and Preteen Boys in Active Literacy*. Newark, DE: International Reading Association.
Brozo, W. G., G. Shiel, and K. Topping. 2008/reissued online 2011. "Engagement in Reading: Lessons Learned from Three PISA Countries." *Journal of Adolescent & Adult Literacy* 51: 4, 304–15.
Donahue, P., M. Daane, and W. Grigg. 2003. *The Nation's Report Card: Reading Highlights 2003*. Washington, DC: National Center for Education Statistics.
Donahue, P. L., K. E. Voelkl, J. R. Campbell, and J. Mazzeo. 1999. *The NAEP 1998 Reading Report Card for the Nation and the States*. Washington, DC: U.S. Department of Education. Office of Educational Research and Improvement. National Center for Education Statistics.
Duke, N. K. 2000. "3.6 Minutes per Day: The Scarcity of Informational Texts in First Grade." *Reading Research Quarterly* 35: 2, 202–24.
Duke, N. K., and V. S. Bennett-Armistead. 2003. *Reading and Writing Informational Text in the Primary Grades: Research-Based Practices*. New York: Scholastic.
Ehri, L. C., L. G. Dreyer, B. Flugman, and A. Gross. 2007. "Reading Rescue: An Effective Tutoring Intervention Model for Language Minority Students Who

Are Struggling Readers in First Grade." *American Educational Research Journal* 44: 2, 414–48.

Goodwin, B., and K. Miller. 2012. "Nonfiction Reading Promotes Student Success." *Educational Leadership* 80–82.

Guthrie, J. T., and N. M. Humenick. 2004. "Motivating Students to Read: Evidence for Classroom Practices that Increase Motivation and Achievement." In P. McCardle and V. Chhabra (Eds.), *The Voice of Evidence in Reading Research*, 329–54. Baltimore: Paul Brookes.

Guthrie, J. T., and A. Wigfield. 2000. "Engagement and Motivation in Reading." In M. L. Kamil, P. Mosenthal, P. D. Pearson, and R. Barr (Eds.), *Handbook of Reading Research*. Vol. 3, 403–22. Mahwah, NJ: Erlbaum.

Hart, B., and T. R. Risley. Spring 2003. "The Early Catastrophe: The 30 Million Word Gap by Age 3." *American Educator*, 4–9.

Ivey, G., and K. Broaddus. 2001. "Just Plain Reading: A Survey of What Makes Students Want to Read in Middle School." *Reading Research Quarterly* 36, 350–77.

Kotaman, H. 2008. "Impacts of Dialogical Storybook Reading on Young Children's Reading Attitudes and Vocabulary Development." *Reading Improvement* 45: 2, 55–61.

Kraemer, L., P. McCabe, and R. Sinatra. 2012. "The Effects of Read-Alouds of Expository Text on First Graders' Listening Comprehension and Book Choice." *Literacy Research and Instruction* 51: 2, 165–78.

Krashen, S. D. 2004. *The Power of Reading: Insights from the Research* (2nd ed.). Santa Barbara: Libraries Unlimited.

National Reading Panel. 2000. *Teaching Children to Read: An Evidence-Based Assessment of the Scientific Research Literature on Reading and Its Implications for Reading Instruction*. Rockville, MD: National Institutes of Child Health and Human Development.

Neuman, S. B. and D. Celano. 2001. "Access to Print in Low-Income and Middle-Income Communities: An Ecological Study of Four Neighborhoods." *Reading Research Quarterly* 36 (1): 8–26.

Neuman, S. B., D. Celano, and N. Moland. 2016. "Book Deserts: The Consequences of Income Segregation on Children's Access to Print." *Urban Education* 0042085916654525, first published on July 5, 2016 as doi:10.1177/00420859 16654525.

Scholastic Inc. and YouGov. 2014. *Kids & Family Reading Report*. scholastic.com/readingreport

Schwartz, G. E. 2002. "Graphic Novels for Multiple Literacies." *Journal of Adolescent & Adult Literacy* 46, 262–65.

———. 2010. "Graphic Novels, New Literacies, and Good Old Social Justice." *The Alan Review* Summer, 71–75.

Sipe, L. R. Feb. 2002. "Talking Back and Taking Over: Young Children's Expressive Engagement during Storybook Read-Alouds." *The Reading Teacher* 55: 5, 476–83.

Swanson, H. L. 1999. "Reading Research for Students with LD: A Meta-Analysis of Intervention Outcomes." *Journal of Learning Disabilities* 32: 6, 504–32.

Teale, W. H., and M. G. Martinez. 1996. "Reading Aloud to Young Children: Teachers' Reading Styles and Kindergartners' Text Comprehension." In C.

Pontecorvo, M. Orsolini, B. Burge, and L. B. Resnick (Eds.), *Children's Early Text Construction*, 321–44. Mahwah, NJ: Erlbaum.

Trelease, J. 2006. *The Read-Aloud Handbook* (6th ed.). New York: Penguin Books.

Yopp, R. H., and H. K. Yopp. 2006. "Informational Texts as Read-Alouds at School and Home." *Journal of Literary Research* 38, 1–37.

Zipoli Jr., R. P., M. D. Coyne, and D. B. McCoach. 2010. "Enhancing Vocabulary Intervention for Kindergarten Students: Strategic Integration of Semantically-Related and Embedded Word Review." *Remedial and Special Education* 32: 2, 131–43.

Chapter 3

Setting Up, Introducing, and Managing Your Classroom Library

Making Your Classroom Library Inviting for Kids

The design of your classroom will send a powerful message to all who enter. Many teachers choose to devote a corner of the classroom to the library, wrapping bookshelves around an area that is also used for whole-class meetings and instruction such as that done in minilessons. The position of your library can convey the message, "This classroom is a place where books and reading are treasured."

You'll want to move heaven and earth to make your classroom library into an inviting place. When creating your classroom library space, borrow lessons from your own reading life. Think of your favorite library or bookstore. What keeps you going back there? Perhaps it is the cozy couches that invite you to explore new titles. Or perhaps you come back because you are drawn in by the ever-changing displays. Are the books grouped by titles and genre, front covers facing outward to catch your eye? You can borrow these ideas for your classroom and create in your own library a space in which the books seem to almost beg to be taken home, just as Corduroy sitting on the shelf at the store seemed to be waiting for Lisa to declare him to be hers for life. The design of your classroom can say to kids, "This library is a special place."

I think back to my own childhood and the places in which I loved to read. These places were cozy and quiet; they felt as they had been designed just for me. I still recall my second-grade teacher who had inexplicably picked up an old bathtub at a tag sale and filled it with pillows. I remember the privilege of being able to climb inside with my stories, knowing that this was a special place where I could devote myself entirely to the sacred act of reading.

You may use stumps, couches, pillows, or low mood lighting to make the classroom library into an inviting place. Add shells or stones or plants or ant farms or stuffed Paddingtons to your library. Hang poems, add art. The message will get through: Books are at the heart of our classroom.

Introduce Your Classroom Library to Kids at the Start of the Year

At the start of the year, you will want to unveil your classroom library with great pomp and circumstance, creating a buzz around this mysterious and wonderful area of your classroom. Ironically, one way to develop the biggest possible drumroll around your classroom library is to keep it off limits for a bit, channeling kids to read from tubs of books until you are ready to make a big deal of the library. To rally their children's excitement about the library, some teachers wrap ribbon around the library until it is ready to be opened and then host a ribbon-cutting ceremony for the official opening.

You might invite kids to meet in the special library you've set up, explaining to them, "We'll meet here often, in our classroom library. Can you see that it's a really important place? See how the bookshelves are arranged. It is like we're wrapped in books—and that is what this year will be like. We are so lucky to have a library like this in our classroom. It's our greatest treasure."

You'll want to play up the role the classroom library will play in your students' reading lives across the year. You might give a mini-keynote address, saying, "You are going to love reading this year—every one of you will. The books in our library aren't just any ol' books. These are books that hundreds and hundreds of teachers, plus kids from all over the world, chose—and they chose these particular books by thinking about just one big thing. They asked themselves, 'What books will make kids *love* reading?'"

You might also say, "Some of these books will teach you about amazing new things: from crazy weather to faraway places. In this library you will encounter monstrously gross and amazing creatures: from slimy sea slugs to big-nosed baboons. You'll also find books about topics that kids know a ton about and grownups do not. You'll find yourself talking about the things you learn in these books, and people will look up and think, 'Are you a genius?'"

As important as fanfare is, it will also be important for you to teach children about the contents and the organizational structure of the library. In the process of developing the TCRWP Classroom Libraries, we visited scores of classrooms to learn in detail about students' preferences. What books did they especially like? What library sections mattered most to them? We were surprised to find that many students often didn't know the breadth of their own classroom libraries and just stuck with a favorite part of the library.

Later in this *Guide*, you'll read about our in logic in creating each shelf of the libraries—and of course, the logic informing the shelves will be very different when the libraries are for beginning readers and for older readers. Some of the information will be important to share with children: Where can they find the alphabet books? The nonfiction books? Many teachers find it is important to give their students library tours, just as one would lead a tour in an art museum, showing off some of the most precious portions.

Your library will change throughout the year as your students learn and grow, but in its earliest moments, you will want to create a space in which students both can and will want to find the books that work for them. Rather than allowing your kids to descend on the shelves willy-nilly, you will probably want to introduce one part of the library, then another. By revealing the contents of the library bit by bit, you can create the sense that there is always something exciting just around the corner for your readers, while also helping your youngsters understand how to find what they want in a library.

> *You and your library have a mission: to put books into your kids' hands and hearts.*
>
>

As the year progresses, you will introduce new portions of the library for new purposes—purposes matched to the work your readers are doing at that time. Early in your kindergarten year, for example, you will want to bring out a few bins filled with small copies of the emergent storybooks that by then you will have read multiple times to the whole class. As kindergarten students move into conventional reading, you will want to introduce bins of pattern books at levels A and B to go with the high-interest storybooks and nonfiction already filling the shelves. Similarly, with first- and second-graders you will probably want to begin the year by showing kids where they can find books that will be just right for them, and then, as children become more accustomed to finding books they can read, you may want to reorganize the library so that books are organized by topic: animal friendships, sports, buddy books.

If you plan on rallying your class around a nonfiction unit of study (and we hope you do) then you may decide to keep some of your most exciting nonfiction books out of sight until the moment comes to display them (not forgetting the fanfare!). In the same way, you might keep a collection of Mo Willems's books out of sight until the time comes to highlight an exciting author study. By withholding some of the books in your library at the start of the year, and then revealing those books when the time is right, you can keep the library feeling fresh and new.

Imbue Your Classroom Culture with a Love of Books

Culture matters. Hang out with kids in the school library, in the cafeteria, on the playground; do this in your school and then in another school, and it will be immediately clear that in each school and classroom, a culture gets established among the student peer group, and that culture wields an incalculable force.

Just as some schools are saturated with an ethic of kindness and others are quite the opposite, so, too, there are "book cultures" in schools where kids collect, swap, and trade books as if they are Pokémon cards (while in other schools, kids grow up feeling as if they'll be ostracized if they are seen with a book). As teacher, you need to assume the role of CEO or guru or whatever title suits you, and you need to rally your students around shared values.

Your Classroom Library is your most important way to grow a positive book culture and to recruit students to love reading, just as you do. You and your library have a mission: to put books into your kids' hands ... and hearts. Your library will help your kids *want* to read and give them access to books. So you will want to develop ways in which the library can be part of an overall classroom culture that inspires kids to read.

Jerry Harste once said, "I see our job as teachers as creating a richly literate world in our classrooms, and then inviting kids to role play their way into being the readers and writers we long for them to become." There is something to Harste's idea that we simply forge ahead, making the classroom and the school into a place that is imbued with a reverence for books, and then we *act* as if students love books as we do. In that environment, students can step into the roles of being strong, passionate readers and writers.

You may also find it beneficial to provide kids with the tools that help them assume the role of being avid readers. The TCRWP Classroom Libraries come complete with tools like reading-level bin labels to help students find their just-right books. For those with complete libraries, small stickers matching the bin-card reading illustrations can be applied to individual books at the teacher's discretion, to support students' ability to independently select and reshelve books. Students can use "reviewer" sticky notes as close-reading lenses that reflect what great readers may think as they read, like "I'm wondering," or "Fun fact!" The Post-its can help them prepare for book discussions and can be left behind to help future readers. Imagine reading along in a book and finding a sticky from a classmate saying "Favorite part!" or "Wow!" You would give those pages extra care, relishing the excitement of the plot and also imagining the excitement of a friend sharing in those words. We think these tools will help you and your students organize your library and then read with greater interest and depth. We hope you and your kids will use these tools as a starting point to help develop and grow your classroom library.

Getting Books into Your Students' Hands— and Keeping Track of Books

Teachers of primary children need to take special care to be sure that kids have access to the library and feel as if it is theirs. The library exists to get books into your kids' hands, but the idea of thirty kindergartners descending upon the classroom library space with baggies in hand, ready to grab up the books they want, can be an overwhelming one.

It will be important for you to think through the details through which children select their books. Many of the teachers with whom we work closely tell students that good readers always have a short stack of "books by the bed" and therefore channel them to select a short stack of books whenever they go to the classroom library. During reading time, children keep that small stack of books at their side, and that stack keeps them in books for at least a few days and hopefully the week. This way, when a reader finishes one book, she can shift to the next without missing a step. How important this is to support children doing a volume of reading! By decreasing the number of trips a reader must make to the classroom library, readers gain more time for reading. Then, too, this means that when you pull up alongside a child, the youngster will have a small collection of books in her baggie, allowing you to think about and talk about the child's work over several days' time.

The number of books that you channel a child to select will vary depending on the child's reading level and the total number of books available. Generally, the idea is that a child fills his or her baggie with enough books to sustain that child's reading for a week. Because books in levels A–E only take a few minutes to read, children reading in those levels need lots of books in their baggies so they can stay engaged during reading time, with the idea that children will reread that stack of books several times each day, and many times across the week.

The books in any of these libraries or shelves alone won't supply you with enough books for your class. They are great starter libraries, but you will need more books. If you are short on books, which is common during your first years with a classroom library, you can economize on books by suggesting that two children who read the same level of books—a matched partnership—select books in tandem and share a baggie of books. If you *really* have too few books, you and another teacher will probably need to wheel book bins between two classrooms.

> *The important thing to convey is that the classroom library is an enduring resource that gives kids access to amazing, incredible books.*
>
>

You will also need to think through a simple and efficient system for your students to check out books. You might consider inviting students to help personalize the classroom checkout system. In the first few days of school, you might provision students with a few half-sheets of white card-stock, and invite them to create their own library checkout markers. Kids illustrate the checkout markers with their names, along with scenes, titles, and lines from their favorite books. You might gather and laminate these cards so they'll stand the test of time. Then, you might teach kids that whenever they check out a book from the library, they must leave one of their checkout markers in the bin from which they got the book. Once a student runs out of checkout markers, she's done selecting books. When it's time to return the books to the library, students simply put a book back in the place of each checkout marker. You may, of course, have other ways to efficiently manage the checkout process in your classroom. (If you have ordered a complete grade-level TCRWP Classroom Library, you will receive details on accessing online resources to accompany the collections, which will include management and sorting data such as book titles, levels, topics, and the like, to help you and your students recreate and keep track of your library resources through many configurations.)

We hope that above all, the message we are conveying is this: There is no one ideal system through which the flow of books can be handled in your classroom. The important thing is that you and your students devote time to creating a system, and that you maintain whatever it is you set into motion, conveying through your diligence that the classroom library is an enduring resource that gives kids—this year and beyond—access to amazing incredible books, and the entire community needs to rally around the job of caring for the library.

Growing Your Library as Your Children Grow

As children grow older and more proficient as readers, they need different books. For example, when a child has just begun kindergarten, before the child has learned that print is read left to right, top to bottom, and before the child knows any letters and sounds, that child won't get a lot out of reading an unfamiliar level A or B book! Instead, such a child would be well off rereading books that you have read aloud, preferably returning to the books you have read often. We refer to the rich storybooks that you have read repeatedly as "emergent storybooks," referencing the research that Elizabeth Sulzby has done about the importance of giving children access to rich, well-structured stories that you have read aloud at least half a dozen times. It is important for children to be invited to approximate-read those books. We've included several copies of a few favorites. Be sure you read aloud those books a few times before you put them out in your classroom library as a resource.

During the early weeks of kindergarten, your students will also learn from books with rich detailed illustrations. At the launch of kindergarten, you might stock tabletop bins with fascinating information books. They'll love to study *National Geographic* magazines and *Where's Waldo* books, too. You will probably be teaching your kindergarten kids about colors, shapes, numbers, and letters, so concept books will be interesting to them as well. The TCRWP Kindergarten Classroom Library includes a few of each of these kinds of texts, and you will want to grow each of these collections so you can give all your students access to books such as these. The good news is that for the first bit of kindergarten, you don't need to search for books that are *both* high interest and easy to read (something that is a bit of a challenge). For a month or two, you needn't worry too much about the books being easy to read (except for the children who arrive in your class already reading), but can just go all out for the high-interest angle.

As the kindergarten school year progresses, you will presumably begin to showcase the leveled texts as your students begin to read levels A, B, C, and so forth. You will probably want to put your level A books into several bins or baskets, not just a single one, since it is hard for children to flip through an overflowing bin. Many teachers advise that you distribute books belonging to a certain level into several bins and only display books that are at levels that are within range for your class at that particular time of year.

First-grade readers grow quickly across the year, and they read books that span a wide range of levels. First-graders often move six to eight reading levels in a year. It will be helpful to get a sense of the students' reading levels from the end of kindergarten, so that you can decide which levels of books—which baskets—to display as you launch the year. For example, if most of your students are reading texts on levels D and E, you will want much of your library to reflect those levels.

You will probably want your leveled bins to include fiction and nonfiction books at each level. As the year progresses, you may move into a nonfiction reading unit,

FIG. 3–1 *As the year progresses in kindergarten, and in first and second grades, you might have a chart hanging in the library area that denotes how many books students at different levels are apt to be shopping for.*

in which case you may want separate bins for nonfiction. If you only have a few nonfiction texts at each level, and students can't fill their baggies with enough nonfiction texts at their level to sustain independent and partner reading, then they will need access to other texts they can read.

In addition to leveled bins, you will want to include nonleveled high-interest texts in your classroom library. We have included some text sets focused on a few particular topics that are enthralling to first-graders, from weather to wild animals to communities and careers. At times, you will want to organize these books by topic rather than by level.

As students enter second grade, those children that are on benchmark will be reading texts in the transitional reading levels. These children will generally move three to five reading levels across the school year. Many of the texts (levels J–N) are early chapter books that are increasing in length and complexity. As you prepare your classroom library, use data on your students' reading levels to decide which bins to feature and which to save for later in the year. Since many of your children will be able to read texts that are longer than those they used to read, second-graders may have fewer books in their baggies—perhaps just five books in a baggie. They'll probably be reading trade books, not the little leveled books that filled their baggies in late kindergarten and for much of first grade. Books that kindergarten teachers read aloud now become mainstays in children's baggies.

Although you will probably still want some books to be filed in leveled bins, by now your children should be fairly good at finding just-right books and at recognizing either an illustrated reading-level label or a color dot that signifies a book's

FIG. 3–2 *It is important to create an efficient system for children to shop for books. Make sure that children are shopping for books outside of the reading workshop to preserve the maximum possible time for actual reading.*

level. Therefore, many second-grade teachers organize books by genre, author, or series.

Second-grade teachers (and many first-grade teachers, too) usually aim to have a nonfiction section to their libraries, with topic-based bins that channel children to read several related books on a topic. Chances are good that there will be a range of reading levels within the bin.

As the year progresses in any of the primary grades, you might have a chart hanging in the library area that denotes how many books students at different levels are apt to be shopping for.

You'll need to decide when you want your children to select their new books—we refer to that as "shopping for books." There is not one perfect time of day for this. Ideally, you will have four to six students shopping on each day of the week, with a posted schedule that gives students ownership over the routine and holds them accountable to their shopping responsibility. The important thing is that you create an efficient system for your students to do this outside of the reading workshop, so that they don't lose precious independent or partner reading time. For example, some teachers suggest that at the start of the school day and at snack time, a few children at a time could be given a chance to return books and gather a new batch.

At the start of the year, students will need to gather their bearings when approaching the library to shop for books. You can support students as they browse the selection of books in a variety of ways. One way you might help students choose just-right books is to do some book or level introductions with them, right on the spot! For example, you could stake a place in the library, choose a few level B texts, and gather some of your level B readers. Amp up their excitement by telling them you found a great book in the bin, maybe read the first page to familiarize them with the pattern, and then hand it over to them to thumb through and keep for the week.

You could also huddle up with your newest level G readers, and bring them to a new bin (and level). You might say to them, "Today is an exciting day. You're now the kinds of readers who are ready for harder books! In this bin, you are going to come across books that are longer than you're used to, and you know what? There will be more things happening in these stories. It will go like this: one thing will happen and then, you keep reading, and . . . another thing happens. And, you read on, and . . . another thing happens. It can get hard to keep track of all the stuff that happens in these longer books, so one thing that helps is—you ready for a tip?—before you start, use the title, the cover, and table of contents to think about what the book will probably be about. Some of these books might even have a blurb on the back you can use." Book introduction and level introductions can lift your students' interest and help orient them to the work they'll be doing.

Once your children have found it easy to find books they can read within the library, you may sort books by topic and interest and not just by level. In addition to the topics we've supplied with complete libaries on illustrated bin cards, you'll want to create your own bins with topics such as "Creepy Bug Books" or "If you liked *Last Stop on Market Street*, you'll like these . . ." or "Room K–309 Favorites." Rally your students to come up with names for new bins, and then use interactive or shared writing to make labels for those bins. Students will feel so proud to have come up with bins like "Chase books" or "Please can I have this pet?" or "BFFs!" or "Tough Times." The titles alone will make these bins into favorites.

Part of book shopping involves returning books from the previous week back to their place in the library before collecting new books. You'll want to teach your students to carefully check a book for any Post-its, bookmarks, or the like, before placing the book with the title facing front, as if on display, in the correct bin. Sometimes, it will be a good idea to leave a particular Post-it in a book for another reader to stumble upon. Other times, your students might remove Post-its from a book when they return the book to the library, storing the best of their Post-its in a special notebook or small photo album.

Building a Sense of Ownership and Community in Your Classroom Library

There are a few ways to imagine how you might strengthen the community and ownership around your classroom library. One of the best ways to show that taking care of books is a class priority is to set aside room in the library for a book hospital. Students will take worn or tattered books—those much-loved, dog-eared, sticky-from-snack-time books in need of attention—to the book hospital for repair. You may want to train a few of your students to be book "doctors" equipped with tape and book repair instruction and put them in charge of getting these books repaired and back into eager hands.

FIG. 3–3 *An illustrated bin card to help students put "lost" books back where they belong.*

Another way to put students at the center of your classroom library is to give a student or group of students the title of class librarian, with the specific responsibility of maintaining the upkeep of the space. The librarians could spend a few minutes organizing books with care, pulling favorites for displays, and sprucing up the area to keep it clean and inviting.

To foster a connection between the library and your children, you might place a bin in your classroom library that is reserved for students' own publications. You might even consider slipping books that students have authored into topic bins where it makes sense to do so. For example, after completing a nonfiction writing unit, you might sort student work into the categories contained in your library, tucking Jamal's "All about Dolphins" book into a Sea Animals bin and Adina's "All about Monster Trucks" into the Transportation bin. Students will beam ear to ear when they stumble across their very own writing featured in the classroom library. They will truly feel that they are part of the library, and the library is very much a part of them.

Refreshing Your Library to Delight and Inspire Children throughout the Year

Just as department stores change their window displays each season, you'll probably want to change your book displays fairly often—to inspire continued interest among readers. At the start of the year, you may display favorites from the prior grade level, surrounding them with related books that your readers will enjoy. In a second-grade classroom, for example, you might prominently display the cover of *I Wanna Iguana* with a sign saying "If you loved *I Wanna Iguana*, then try . . ." next to several appropriate books. Later, you might feature nonfiction bins around the topics you are studying in the content areas: community helpers, plants and gardens, farm animals. Other times, you may want to showcase new series books or books themed around an upcoming season or holiday. Always, when you group books together, you encourage kids to do the important work of reading more deeply and developing in-depth interests.

Interestingly, we learned the importance of keeping libraries fresh from the Teachers College's Center for Infants and Toddlers. The professor who leads that center once explained to us that you can tell the quality of a preschool by the emphasis it places on storage. "On storage?" we asked, amazed. Annette explained that the wrong thing to do with young kids is to put all the toys out in the room at the same time, keeping it all out for the year, making the room feel like a giant toy box. For the first week, kids will be on overload, playing for five minutes with one toy, then the next, then the next. Within two weeks, they will have raced through all the surface-level fun activities that the toys suggest, and they'll feel bored. How much better to strategically release a few at a time, choosing ones that combine in a variety of ways: a slide, a truck, a few blocks (imaginary trucks), a cloth, a few stuffed animals. Just that handful of items can inspire lots of thoughtful play.

Similarly, you will want to save some of the really fascinating books in your library for later, knowing that they can launch a new line of work. When one of those books is brought forward, it can be prominently displayed and you can read bits of it aloud. That way each book will have a chance to work its magic.

Over time, your library will come to reflect your students and their ever-evolving interests, passions, and identities. If lots of your students are taking swimming lessons, you might want to create a bin all about swimming, famous swimmers, even the Olympic games. When you notice that all the Mercy Watson books have flown off your shelves, you'll create a new basket, "Cousins to Mercy Watson: Hilarious Chapter Books!" Similarly, when your kids come back buzzing with excitement from a visit to the aquarium, you might craft a basket called "Everything Underwater," including books about everything from jellyfish to scuba divers. These evolving book bins will keep interest in the library high and allow you a chance to advertise some of the books your youngsters might otherwise miss.

You may also decide to feature your read-alouds for the month, allowing students to revisit those texts independently. The books we read aloud to students often become classroom favorites and are worth talking more about, so displaying those texts and encouraging children to reread them is a good idea. Then, too, you may want to highlight shared reading favorites, probably asking students to take them out for just a few minutes at a time so you'll always have familiar shared reading texts on hand to which you can return.

Those display shelves can also hold copies of the books found tucked inside leveled baskets. You might, on occasion, introduce these little books to grow excitement and interest among your readers. It's amazing what a book on a shelf can encourage a reader to do. Whatever your decision, making the library belong to the community is key.

In addition, you may highlight and bring attention to those books that support your current units of study in reading, writing, and the content areas. Reading affects every part of our life, so our classroom library should do that same work. If you are studying weather patterns in science, for example, make space in the library for weather books to live together.

You can also choose to make certain books "famous" by bringing attention to them across different parts of your day and in your library displays. Perhaps you pull some of your favorite level D books, and read them aloud to the class, highlighting that you found them in your very own classroom library! Students will be eager to read not only those books, but also to scavenge the rest of the bins for their own golden treasures to keep in their baggies.

Tools for the TCRWP Classroom Libraries

Witty, Wise, and Whimsical Tools

Presentation matters. Stick a daisy between the soap and the dishwashing fluid alongside your kitchen sink and that flower looks like No Big Deal. Place the same flower in a tiny vase, set it at the center of your table, perhaps with a bit of white lace under the vase, and you're well on the way toward re-creating the Metropolitan Museum of Art.

Presentation matters for readers, too. When studying classroom libraries prior to launching this endeavor, we were stunned to see how many enthralling books were overlooked simply because they were jammed into bins titled simply "Nonfiction" or "Science."

But of course libraries must not only be appealing places, they must also be accessible. You'll find that with your complete grade-level library, we've included tools and resources to help get you and your students started creating engaging and inviting instructional and organizational materials.

Book Bin Label Cards: Categorizing Books in Intriguing Ways

Visit any bookstore and watch customers—readers—for just a few minutes. It will immediately be apparent to you the importance of categorizing books, putting them into shelves and baskets that are labeled in quirky or provocative ways in order to entice readers. Think of the millions of dollars this nation has spent trying to motivate kids to read—and all that was needed (well, not all, but a good start) was for the books to be categorized in intriguing ways. Imagine, for example, a bin

titled "Wild Weather" containing books about lightning storms, types of clouds, and even tornadoes. What wonderful conversations readers will have about the weather happening all around them.

The TCRWP counts itself lucky to have on its staff talented illustrators, who have made a starter set of bin labels that may help you group your books: "Emergent Storybooks," "Alphabet Books," "Concept Books," and "Songs and Poems." These heavy card-stock labels are just the beginning. If you have not selected a complete library, and/or as your students become more familiar with your library and its contents, they may want to create their own additional labels. Perhaps your first-graders will discover several intriguing books on different countries and cultures within your leveled bins. They might then create their own new bin titled "Dream Trips" filled with books on places they'd love to visit. This will give children that wonderful feeling of being part of the curation of their own library.

Book Level Labels: Offering Accessibility

Much of the work done in the early reading years is focused on matching children to "just-right" books, or books matched at or just above their current reading ability. You may, therefore, want to create leveled book bins, perhaps at the beginning of the school year, for the majority of your books. This strategy will make just-right books easily accessible for even the youngest readers. (We discuss leveling in much greater detail in Chapter 5.) Should you choose to go this route, you will want to label each individual book with its level so that students can easily rehome books as needed. We have provided miniature level labels to match the illustrated bin cards for this purpose. Reshelving of books then becomes a job that students can take on as part of their book-shopping routines or, again, you might specifically assign a team of "classroom librarians" or "bibliographers" to head up this aspect of library maintenance.

Other teachers may choose not to share lettered reading levels with students, but might color code books by text complexity to make just-right text accessible, but allow kids to expand their reading lives beyond the confines of level. In this case, you will also want to label your books, but instead of affixing the letter C to cover, you might choose to label levels C through D with the color blue and have readers across this text band select books from within that color label.

At times you will want to mix up books across different levels. You might, for example, put together a range of autumn-themed texts for your readers to peruse in the month of October or collect books about sea creatures as your class prepares for a field trip to the aquarium. In this case, having students be able to identify books that will be accessible is key to their success. Having level or color-coded stickers will make this an easy proposition and will help students quickly predict if a certain book might be too hard, too easy, or just right.

Book Management Data

Included with each shelf of books is a title-by-title list, including topic and level for each book. For those who have chosen a full grade-level Classroom Library, complete library lists are also provided in the online resources, to assist with managing, tracking, and stickering your books. (A separate card is provided in the grade-level Classroom Libraries Tools and Resources box, which provides detailed online resource registration information and instructions.)

Student Sticky-Note Pads: Supporting a Variety of Reading

You will also see that with complete grade-level libraries we've given you a collection of Post-it notepads that students can use with their books as they read and think. Our goal has been to create notes that say something that great readers often think as they read: "Wow!" or "Tricky word!" or "Whoa, this is deep!" When kids use these stickies while they read, you'll see that they tend to read more alertly. Post-it notes, then, can act as lenses to support close, active reading.

We expect that readers will usually leave notes on pages as a quick-jot to flag favorites and call out "must-reads" for others, or most importantly, as a way to remind themselves to return to those pages during their partner conversation—to support their thinking, talking, and writing about the book. Readers may also decide to leave some of the stickies in a book as tips for future readers. Picture a reader pausing at the end of a book to decide where to put a few keynotes for future readers, perhaps going back and putting a "Favorite part!" at the beginning of a chapter they just read. Picture another reader asking herself which pages merit the "Important!" Post-it. As with the bin labels, these sticky notes are just the start.

They are a jumping-off point for your readers to create their own stickies to expand their thinking. Of course, if you did not select a complete library, you and your students can always make their own jots with blank sticky notes. Whether you're creating all your own, or adding to the sticky-note collection you've received, you'll want to explicitly introduce various types of sticky notes to your students.

To launch the "favorite" jots sticky notes, you might model using these Post-its for your students. Perhaps you just finished reading *Tales of Bunjitsu Bunny* by John Himmelman. You might gather your readers and say, "Readers, I have to share with you that I loved *Tales of Bunjitsu Bunny* and I've been thinking about how we need a system for letting our classmates know when we love a book and think others might love it too. So, I found [or *made*] these Post-its that are just perfect for the job. I'll stick this 'I give this book 5 stars!' jot on the cover and sign my name so others will know that in my opinion this book is a must-read." After this, you'll want to make this Post-it and others like it available to students so that they can highlight the books they love for their classmates.

To introduce the sticky notes that are "tips to future readers," you might carry them in your conferring toolkit and share them with students as the opportunity arises. If a reader says to you, "You know at first I thought this book was a real dud, but now I can't put it down." You could respond with, "Wow. That is so incredibly thoughtful of you because you are thinking, perhaps without even knowing it, about future readers of this book and what they might need to know. I've got just the jot for you!" It's important to be mindful of not making our teaching too small, too narrow. So you might also say, "Here are a few other 'tips to future readers' jots that you can have on deck as you read. And, knowing you, you'll invent some even better tips that we'll need to add into this collection."

Finally, there are jots that promote thinking, talking or writing about books with others. You'll want to use these in a similar fashion to the 'tips to future readers" jots. That is, have them on hand and introduce them in your conferring or small-group work. Imagine you've got a group of readers who need support connecting the parts of a text into a cohesive whole. You might say, "Readers, I've

been thinking about the books that you are reading and the thinking work you are doing in those books and I realized that one thing that might really pay off for you is to think about how parts of the text fit together or connect." After practicing this work on a shared text, you might add, "One trouble with small-group work can be that we don't transfer what we just practiced into our independent book reading, so check this out, let's keep these Post-its on hand as we read so we'll remember to practice this work in our independent books." Readers might then go on to share this thinking in their own books, leaving notes for future readers such as "Tricky Word!" or "Life Lesson Learned Here!" which will, in turn, cause others to pause and take on new thinking.

It's inspiring to see kids read with extra alertness, noticing things they wouldn't have noticed otherwise. When you put these notes in play with kids, you'll see something interesting happen. Almost immediately, kids begin to suggest other stickies that they believe deserve to be out in the world. Soon the class will be at work making many of its own sticky notes—as well as reading with new lenses.

Chapter 4

What's in the TCRWP Classroom Libraries?

Curating the K–2 Classroom Libraries

We use the term *curating* to describe our work building these K–8 classroom libraries because we have aimed to do the kind of high-quality and high-interest work that curators do at the Metropolitan Museum of Art.

The truth is, the contents of your classroom library matter very much. The books you put before your students will affect the readers they become. If you want the young people in your care to grow up accustomed to discovering an author and then reading more and more books by that person, then your library needs to make that likely. If you want young people to fall in love with a character, and then to read, rooting for that character, learning from her, weeping when she is hurt, then your library needs to make that sort of deep involvement with a character possible—even inevitable. If you want young people to grow up, expecting to experiment with new kinds of texts, the books you put before them can support that adventurous spirit. So, too, your library can teach your children that the world is endlessly fascinating, that a rotten log or a drop of river water can be endlessly intriguing, that families come in all shapes and sizes, that the stories of history are full of drama and courage. The next generation can grow up expecting that the simple act of putting books into bins and titling those bins can invite grand conversations and spark rereading. We fret over feeding children nourishing food, yet too often act as if one book is interchangeable with another. A carefully chosen library is as important to the health of a child as is a carefully chosen menu of nutritious food.

Our goal has been to create libraries for kids that are perfectly aligned to reading development and that will provide youngsters with a pathway that enables them to read increasingly complex books over time. We have been careful to supply them with books that are both high quality and high interest.

Know that for each book we have included, we considered at least a score of other books (and often twice that many)—all books that also came with strong recommendations. We took the goal of locating high-interest books very seriously. We literally brought finalists home to our own kids and our friends' kids, and asked, "Look these books over and tell me which you want to read." We sat in classrooms, asking readers, "Which books in this classroom will get other kids to love reading as much as you do?" Our fingers couldn't type fast enough to capture all their suggestions!

To achieve this balance, we relied upon perspectives and opinions of people who have different priorities. Anita Silvey, the former editor of the prestigious children's literature journal, *The Horn Book*, who was a great source of guidance for the grades 3–8 libraries, points out, "The remarkable thing about the TCRWP Classroom Libraries project is that so many different perspectives have been brought to bear on selecting the books." She is right. For each book, we considered if the book would lure a reader to read, if it would be rewarding when read, and if it would provide readers with the right mix of supports and challenges.

That means we also asked, "Will this book help kids develop skills as powerful readers?" The considerations we made in response to that question are partly detailed in the extensive discussion in Chapter 5 of the leveling work we undertook as part of curating these libraries.

In every part of the Classroom Libraries, we considered issues of representation and diversity. We know that all children long for and deserve to see themselves represented in the books in their classroom. We also know that a single book can unwittingly make a stereotype of an identity, or seem a token inclusion. We strove, therefore, with advice from as many experts as possible, to provide texts that celebrate multiple perspectives, cultures, histories, and identities.

> *We considered if each book would lure a reader, be rewarding, and provide supports and challenges.*

A note about shelves in the K–2 Classroom Libraries. We built the K–2 libraries by curating shelves, a process that involved a team of people including all of the K–2 staff developers at TCRWP plus many others. When building libraries for young readers, our first priority was to provision kids with as many little leveled books of high interest and high quality as possible, because we know a young reader can read and reread a stack of ten level C books in a day. Yes, that child will relish the chance to return to those books, rereading them and seeing more in them, but it is also critical that there are many more level C books—and that a similar repository exists for subsequent levels of text complexity. For this reason, a big percentage of the K–2 library consists of shelves containing the very best on-level books we could find for levels A–N.

We have also created shelves to meet particular curricular needs. For the youngest readers, for example, the library includes the Concept Books shelf to teach basic concepts such as ABCs, counting, and colors, while providing opportunities for your children to learn to distinguish between pictures and print, and to learn that pages of a book go together to tell about a topic. For emergent readers, the library includes the Emergent Storybooks shelf to support your kindergartners as they expand their knowledge of how a story goes and learn important reading behaviors on their path toward conventional reading. As children move from reading little leveled books to chapter books in levels J–M, you may wish to extend your

library with the Series Book Club shelf. These shelves are discussed in greater detail later in this chapter.

Anyone who has taught in a wide range of schools knows that the term *grade-level reading* is an optimistic term. At one point, the term probably referred to the *average* level at which children at a particular grade could read by the end of that grade-level year. Increasingly, however, our competitive, standards-based society has been raising the bar. Levels of text complexity that were once expected in late fourth grade are now being expected in mid-second grade. Raising the bar might be a great idea if the rise in expectations had been accompanied by an increase in funding for professional development and for classroom libraries—the two things that can actually lift the level of children's work. Nationally, most new funding for reading has been swallowed up by the very costly effort to rewrite the assessments and the related press to provision schools with the technology on which those tests are being given.

Because expectations have risen and yet many kids haven't progressed, there is an increasingly large gap between the level at which many children can actually read and the levels of text complexity that match "grade-level expectations." Consequently, many kids who need to be reading ravenously if they are going to regain lost ground as readers aren't given books that are within their zones of proximal development.

The good news is that once a reader is given a book that he or she can actually read with high levels of accuracy, fluency, and comprehension—once reading actually clicks for that child—then readers can often progress quickly. For this reason, it is especially important that children who are reading well below benchmark have access to books they can read—and books they *want* to read. For these students we have created a Below-Benchmark Library for each grade in grades 1–8. The Below-Benchmark Grade 1 Library is not simply the kindergarten library repackaged. Instead, we considered the age level as well as the reading level of below-benchmark readers, and we chose as wide a range as possible of enticing and accessible books. Curating the Below-Benchmark shelves required exponentially more time than other aspects of this endeavor.

The Process of Curating a Specific Shelf

The entire staff of the Project worked shoulder-to-shoulder to review, level, organize, and rank the thousands and thousands of books that we reviewed. We categorized the incoming books, made plans for the number of books and distribution of book levels that we believed should comprise a particular shelf, and above all, we read, read, and read some more.

For every grade level, we have data on tens of thousands of kids' reading levels and the levels of text complexity at which they are reading. We used that data to help decide how many books at each level of text complexity were needed for classrooms reading roughly at benchmark levels, and also for classrooms in which kids are reading well below benchmark levels.

For example, for a grade 1 benchmark library (intended for a teacher whose students are mostly reading at grade level, with some below and some above grade level), research in reading levels suggests a plan like this:

Grade 1 Benchmark Library (739 Books)

Book Bin	Number of Books
Read-Aloud and Poetry	26
Shared Reading	15 titles, 4 copies ea.
Level C	49
Level D	77
Level E	76
Level F	74
Level G	58
Level H	70
Level I	77
Level J	62
Level K	54
Level L	56

For each of the grade-level shelves, special insights emerged regarding content that also shape the design of each shelf. In the sections that follow and in Chapter 5 "Leveling Books, Assessing Students, and Matching Readers to Books," we crystalize some of those insights.

The Read-Aloud Shelves

Think about the times when you have been utterly swept up by a read-aloud. Perhaps you were the teacher, reading the book to your kids. You may remember the intensity with which they listened, the way you could turn a page, pause, look at them, and then, slowly, begin to read aloud, knowing there wasn't one child who wasn't absolutely hanging on your every word. Perhaps, when you think about the read-aloud books that have mattered most, your memories stretch back to when your mom or dad read to you. For Molly, it's a black-and-white picture book about three brothers riding a pinto pony; she remembers dreaming about that pony, where she would keep it, how she'd care for it.

You won't be surprised to hear that we spent days, weeks, months, choosing the books that we feature in the read-aloud shelves in the TCRWP Classroom Libraries. After all, these books need to have the power to draw kids in. They also need to change the values, the conversations, in a classroom in that special way that books can, making everyone more wide-awake, more generous, more ready to laugh and forgive and to work with joy.

Choosing read-alouds was especially challenging because when we asked our 600-plus expert consultants to send along book recommendations, the people who sent K–2 titles almost never sent us the title to a little leveled book, nor did they send us titles to chapter books. The vast majority of recommendations were for picture books. How to choose just twenty of those for each grade level's read-aloud shelf? How to choose just twenty for inclusion in each of our libraries? The competition was to say the least, intense.

We're wildly excited about the books we did finally select. We're sure that you and your second-graders will enjoy *President Squid* by Aaron Reynolds, the story of a pretentious squid with presidential aspirations whose zany "five reasons why I should be president" will keep your students rolling with laughter. However, we chose *President Squid* not only because we know it will make your second-graders laugh, but also because recent reforms in the teaching of writing have highlighted the importance of opinion writing, and we know that throughout the world, children as young as kindergartners and certainly second-graders are writing reviews, persuasive letters, and petitions. They, like President Squid, need to persuade an audience.

You and your kindergartners will fall in love with the curmudgeonly old bear Bruce in Ryan T. Higgins's *Mother Bruce*. When Bruce goes to make a gourmet omelet, his eggs unexpectedly hatch into three little gosling chicks. "I am NOT your mother," Bruce says to the baby geese who want to follow him everywhere. You won't be surprised to learn that Bruce changes, even taking the chicks on their annual southern migration by bus since he cannot fly. Again, we chose this book not only because you and your kids will fall in love with this very funny little family, but also because Bruce goes through huge changes, and the book will help you to teach your little ones the basics of narrative craft. It is a perfectly shaped problem-solution story, with a character who does indeed change.

In choosing the books that would comprise the read-aloud shelves, we wanted also to provide you with a forum for having deep and important conversations with your kids. We wanted to offer you picture books that deserve to be returned to often and that could teach lessons about life. In Matt de la Peña's 2016 Newbery Award Winner, *Last Stop on Market Street*, young CJ is full of all the things he thinks he must have: an iPod, a family car, a cleaner neighborhood. His grandmother takes him to the last stop on the Market Street bus where there is a soup kitchen, and the two of them volunteer together. It will not only be CJ, but also the kids in your class, who leave that time at the soup kitchen rethinking whether they do, in fact, need all the trinkets that had once seemed so all-important.

We're also excited for your first-graders to hear Pat Zietlow Miller's *The Quickest Kid in Clarksville*. They will love meeting Alta, a young girl who longs to race like her hometown hero Wilma Rudolph, the Olympic hero. Alta is the quickest kid in Clarksville until a new girl comes to town, one with shiny new shoes. Alta begins to worry about her ragged old sneakers—and her position as the town's best runner. The two girls eventually realize that they both idolize Wilma Rudolph, and they come together around their shared hero, and in the process, they learn (and teach) something important about friendship.

Nonfiction—both narrative and expository—constitutes a third of each read-aloud collection. We've chosen books that will support kids in doing the nonfiction reading work that you're probably teaching them to do during your reading mini-lessons. You'll be able to use your read-aloud as a way to apprentice kids in thinking about and assembling all the information on a page, including that contained in pictures and diagrams as well as in words. You'll also use these books to teach kids that when reading nonfiction, readers learn a bit about a new word, and then they read on, and learn more and more about that one same word, coming over time to a deep understanding of it. A child might learn a bit about migration on page 1, but then on later pages, all of a sudden she comes to grasp the true mystery of monarch butterflies winging their way across the continent.

When choosing the nonfiction books to read aloud, we were aware that we were choosing topics as well as books, and we made choices deliberately. We wanted to provide kids with books that helped them to experience that lightbulb-going-on experience of a dawning idea. We wanted books that would help them think, "Oh my gosh, I never knew that! Holy moly, that is coooooool!" For this reason, we selected some books that we imagine will revisit topics the kids know well, bringing new illumination to those topics. Children will be amazed to hear, when you read them *Surprising Sharks* by Nicola Davis, that sharks aren't the dangerous hunters they see on TV, but instead are amazing animals that have more to fear from us than we do from them.

We also chose some books on topics we figured kids might not even know existed. Who would have thought that some people have the job of being a street cleaner, for example? Who would have thought that dragonflies catch their prey by making a net out of their many legs?

Of course, nonfiction books, like fiction books, convey values, and we tried to select books that value the habits of mind that we know you value as well. We chose books that say to kids, "There is nothing better in all of life than having a job you love. It is such a privilege to work hard on a project that makes a difference in the world." For that reason, we included Jennifer Berne's *On a Beam of Light: A Story of Albert Einstein* and Andrea Davis Pinkney's *Duke Ellington: The Piano Prince and His Orchestra*. Then, too, we wanted books that say to kids, "The hard things in life make us stronger. Whatever is hard for you—just remember, that can end up making you stronger." We know you and your kids will have conversations about that after you read and reread Alan Rabinowitz's autobiography *A Boy and a Jaguar*. The book starts

with six-year-old Alan, afraid to talk to other kids or to his teacher because of a terrible stutter. Alan finds that he is only comfortable talking to his cat and his rabbit, because he knows they won't laugh at his stutter. Animals become a source of solace for Alan, and he resolves that when he grows up, he'll find a way to give back to them. In the end, Alan becomes an important advocate for animal conservation worldwide.

The Shared Reading Shelves

Shared reading provides a powerful link between the direct instruction of read-aloud and the work your students are doing on their own during independent reading. While going through the mountains of leveled books that could potentially be used in shared reading library shelves, we were incredibly particular in selecting the books that actually made the cut. These are books that your class will adore and want to go back and read over and over again.

When selecting books for shared reading, we chose books that would be slightly above where the majority of students would likely be reading. Because of this, the shelves of shared reading titles in the below-benchmark libraries look quite different from those in the benchmark libraries. For example, while the beginning of the year benchmark in second grade is I/J, which means that readers progressing on course will be reading those levels and those who are working substantially below grade level will not yet be tackling those levels, we nevertheless envision that much of your shared reading at that tier will engage your kids in the more challenging work of reading books that are classified as being at levels K and L.

Of course, the shared reading books differ by grade level. Kindergartners will love the rhyming, sing-songy words of Joy Cowley's *Wishy Washy Clothes* and Sue Williams's *I Went Walking*. Even after you have taught these books, you will want to bring them back time and time again to serve as warm-ups as your students take on higher-level texts. You may also want to draw warm-ups from the familiar nursery rhymes found in Sylvia Long's *Mother Goose* anthology, as well as from the familiar charts and posters around your classroom.

Within the kindergarten and first-grade shelves, you will also find more traditional books such as Olivier Dunrea's *Gossie* and Jenny Giles's *Little Chimp Finds Some Fruit*. These books are particularly supportive of the word-solving work that students are doing between levels C and G. Each of these books provides kids with several words that will be challenging and yet can be solved by readers relying on multiple sources of information (Reading Recovery MSV). These books are also written in such a way that even in a first reading, children will be chiming in with your reading. On subsequent reads, they will be able to work with more depth on the word work and comprehension opportunities these books provide.

As students grow and texts become longer and more complex, you may decide to use the books from this shelf in different ways. When engaging kids in shared reading of stories like Kate DiCamillo's *Mercy Watson to the Rescue*, you will want to project enlarged versions of some of the chapters so they support shared reading and meanwhile, you'll want to use other chapters for a more traditional read-aloud. This will allow students to enjoy and learn from the entire story, while also zooming in on specific parts.

You will also want to take a similar approach to the higher-level nonfiction texts in the shared reading shelves. With high-interest topics like tornadoes and spiders, you might choose to read the entire text aloud to students and then return to a section or two, this time using shared reading as a way to engage students in taking a closer look at the vocabulary, text structure, and content of that portion of the text. As students join you in a shared reading of expository text, you will probably want to remind them that they should sound like the voice heard in many documentary television shows—in other words, the reader assumes a teaching voice when reading expository nonfiction texts.

Always during shared reading, you will want students to jump right in, reading along with you. Plan to take the lead on particularly tricky parts of the text. Then return to those texts, again inviting students to join you. You will be amazed by how quickly your students' fluency will improve within each text. As you plan, you will find that shared reading is most powerful when the focus is closely aligned to the skills that students most need to strengthen.

After a text is used for shared reading, you will want many students to carry over this book to their independent reading to keep practicing that great fluency and word-solving work independently. Therefore, we have included four copies of these shared reading texts so that multiple students can continue to work with a text after you have used it with the full class.

Concept Books (Kindergarten)

Tucked into the kindergarten libraries is a shelf of concept books. These books do not contain plot or characters, but rather all center on familiar, engaging topics: ABC's, counting, and colors. In these books, your kindergartners will practice reading cover to cover, distinguishing between pictures and print, and learn that pages of a book go together to tell about a topic. As your students read and reread, they will think more about what's on each page—categorizing and learning more about a topic. They will talk to friends and teachers about the book and build a richer vocabulary. For example, while reading Cathryn Falwell's *Feast for 10*, your kindergartners will explore numbers up to ten while also bolstering vocabulary around grocery shopping and food. Similarly, in *Colorful Days*, readers will build a stronger language base around color, while also saying more and more about all different-colored things. These books will show your youngest readers that they can learn more about their world within the pages of a book by "reading" the pictures; these books will also provide fodder for enthusiastic practice in talking about books with peers and adults.

Emergent Storybooks (Kindergarten)

It's important to support kindergarten children in using their knowledge of stories to support their reading. Elizabeth Sulzby's work on what she refers to as "emergent storybook reading" allows teachers to provision kindergarten students with books that they have heard read aloud so many times that the children announce, "I can read that book with my eyes closed." Sulzby's research suggests that it is very important for adults to read some rich stories to children over and over, in a way that resembles that "bedtime" read-aloud, and then children need opportunities to "read" those books themselves, storytelling their way through them.

You will recognize many familiar books as you dive into the emergent storybooks in your kindergarten library shelf. When selecting books for this shelf, we prioritized stories that follow a conventional story structure and have illustrations that clearly match the words on each page. Stories with repeating lines and/or plot are often easier for students to retell. In this shelf you'll see old favorites such as *Corduroy*, *The Three Billy Goats Gruff*, *The Carrot Seed*, and *Harry the Dirty Dog*. These are stories you will want to read to students again and again, and once your kindergartners have heard a story several times, you will want to give them a chance to "read" the stories on their own. This reading will not be conventional, though you will want to call it "reading" nonetheless. With each reading, your students will reread or retell as best they can, building up story language and important reading behaviors. As they read, they will expand their knowledge of how a story goes and build a strong vocabulary.

Series Book Clubs (Grade 2)

In second grade, your students will be tackling texts at higher levels of text complexity, moving into books on levels J–K and L–M. At this time, your students will begin moving away from little leveled readers and will begin accessing more and more commercially available books, like those you might pick up at a bookstore. As students enter these levels, series books play an important role in your kids' reading development. Series books are highly patterned. Once your kids can read one book in a series, they will see how the series goes and can predict what to expect in the others. In Magic Tree House books, for example, everything is the same. Each time, Jack and Annie get into the tree house, read a book, and have an adventure. Jack is scared; Annie is not. Your kids can use the schema they've already built to jump into these texts.

While some students will want to (and should) read through a series independently, you may also want to set aside a part of this shelf for use in series book clubs. These small series shelves give you a taste of some really great series that provide ample room for thinking and discussion.

Rather than include entire series, think of these as starter sets. You may want to buy additional copies of certain titles so that partnerships can read a title together, or you may want to buy additional books in the series that your students really love, expanding your collection of several Katie Woo titles to include a much wider array.

Curating Libraries for Very Young Readers: Knowing the Publishers

It was a different process to curate the TCRWP Classroom Libraries for very young readers than to do the same work for older readers. When we asked literacy experts and teachers for their all-time favorite must-have books, we received few recommendations for level C and D books. When we searched websites on books, read blogs on books, sought out the award-winning books, we found this didn't tend to produce lists of all-star little leveled books. The best books for kindergarten and first-grade readers aren't highlighted at the local bookstore, nor even passed from teacher to teacher. People tend not blog about these books, nor do they appear on national award lists.

When we invited teachers and literacy leaders to recommend their favorite titles for K–2 readers to us, we found that they were much more likely to recommend particular *publishers* rather than particular titles. So we set about locating the best publishers of K–2 books. Again, we tapped the knowledge of early literacy experts from around the country. We studied the contents of the K–2 libraries we especially admired. We attended national conferences and, for the first time in our lives, skipped every session to live in the conference halls, studying the booksellers and their wares.

We found that for K–2, teachers and literacy leaders were more likely to recommend publishers, rather than particular books.

We found that teachers in different parts of the country tend to champion different publishers. Teachers in New York City raved about Pioneer Valley's nonfiction and series books, while our colleagues in Louisiana and California guided us to Townsend Press's great fiction for early readers. Pockets of teachers swore by Sundance, others loved Hameray Publishing Group. Teachers who have worked with TCRWP know of and appreciate books from Kaeden Books because they are essential to our K–2 assessments. On the whole, our sense is that knowledge of great publishers in the K–2 grades has generally spread more slowly than knowledge of great books in the upper grades. Still, when you combine knowledge, it's not hard to soon be surrounded by wonderful books from MaryRuth Books, RR Books, Okapi Educational Materials, Benchmark Education, Candlewick Press, Kaeden, National Geographic Children's Books, Children's Press, Curriculum Press, DK Publishing, Educators Publishing Service, Keep Books, Lee & Low Books, Mondo Publishing, Newbridge, Richard C. Owen, Rigby, Scholastic, Sundance, Sunshine Books from New Zealand, and other publishers.

It is quickly apparent that no publisher is equally strong in everything. It is helpful to know the particular strengths of different publishers. And certainly, classroom libraries need to draw on many publishers for children to be given a balanced reading diet. Many publishers feature a few authors who write scores of books. Many have their own standard format. Kids deserve to read books that have been published by a wide variety of publishers. Just as you wouldn't want to wear only Laura Ashley clothing to every occasion, youngsters deserve to be exposed to a wide range of books.

One of the great advantages of the TCRWP Classroom Libraries is that the books are drawn from lots and lots of publishers, and in each instance, we have made an enormous effort to tap the special strengths of each publisher. The books will do the best possible job of introducing you to publishers, and we know you'll go directly to the publishers you love for more of their books, but we also thought it might help if we gave you just a few "If . . . , Then . . ." highlights and a quick list (see the end of this section) to help you get to know many of these great K–2 publishers.

If your readers have been in the beginning stages for a long time and need carefully leveled and especially supportive books . . .

Children who are beginning readers for a long while—who are not progressing as one might wish—will benefit from especially well-structured and highly supportive texts. For these readers, texts need to take into account all that is known about reading development, and they also need to be as high-interest as possible, without throwing challenges at readers that will derail them. If you teach kids with these needs, we'd suggest that you populate your library especially with books published by Rigby.

The important thing to stress is that if you have diverse readers who are not catching on with reading, it can be tempting to draw especially from publishers whose niche is publishing books with diverse characters. But as important as multicultural literature is—and we think it is very important—readers who are having

trouble getting traction really benefit from books in which the levels are precisely right—books that are written to be supportive in ways that match kids' needs.

We especially value a particular line of PM books from Rigby that was written decades ago and has recently been given a contemporary makeover; the Rigby Platinum Edition. Look also for the Rigby series books, such as *In the Days of the Dinosaurs* and *Little Chimp*. Other classic books that were once published by the Wright Group are now available from Sunshine Books New Zealand.

If your goal is to put super-engaging nonfiction texts into kids' hands, and to especially give kids texts that have lots of supportive text features . . .

There are a number of good possibilities in this category. We are especially enthusiastic about two series from Pioneer Valley: Explore the World and Discover Our World. We find these series of books provide strong text supports for readers navigating the increasingly complex demands of nonfiction, while also engaging reluctant readers in unique, high-interest topics such as jellyfish, horse therapy, and snowboarding. The photographs in Pioneer Valley nonfiction books are especially gorgeous.

Newbridge (which is linked to Sundance) also provides nonfiction texts that your kids will find engaging. Think of this publisher as an especially strong source of books you can use for shared reading of content-specific topics. They provide small copies of their big books.

If you want to help readers grow theories about characters, even when their books are for beginning readers . . .

If you are teaching from the TCRWP Units of Study series, there are particular publishers that will be your go-to places for books that support the specific work in the units. For example, when you want to support your young readers to do some deep thinking about characters, you may turn to Hameray's beautiful collection of Joy Cowley books. These books will be at the top of our list for books that are perfect for shared reading.

Joy Cowley has been a beloved author for decades. The collections of her books published by Hameray give a fresh look to some of our favorites—Mrs. Wishy-Washy and friends and Dan the Flying Man—while introducing us to new adventures and even new characters. Hameray texts are also supportive and consistent.

Pioneer Valley also has engaging characters, and one of the great things about their character books is that often the same character appears in texts that are more or less complex. The characters in this line of books include Quack the Duck, Bella and Rosie, Jasper the Cat, Marvin Pig, Princess Pig, and Gilbert the Pig, to name a few.

Kaeden Books has a series of books centered on a mischievous, playful dog named Sammy. This series of books covers many levels, and there are new titles in publication that will feature Sammy stories at higher levels (e.g., levels J and K). Kaeden also offers a series of books with the same characters that centers on members of a family's adventures while fishing.

All of these publishers feature engaging characters in well-written and supportive texts.

If you don't have much money and want to use every penny well . . .

We're wildly enthusiastic about Candlewick's Brand New Readers series, which is an inexpensive series of books that are perfect for supporting comprehension and inferencing work, even at low levels (C, D) where many texts don't ask for as much thinking. Candlewick publishes Kate DiCamillo and many lively, quirky, thoughtful, well-written texts for upper-grade readers, so it is nice to see that even at those low levels, Candlewick has managed to publish stories that are funny, have lively illustrations, and provoke thoughtful responses.

You might be familiar with some of their characters—Ethan, Worm, Mouse, and Piggy and Dad—just to name a few. The characters are featured in lots of their texts and series.

Keep Books, published by the Ohio State University, are also very inexpensive and feature a wide variety of high-interest titles at reading levels appropriate for Pre-K through grade 2. Keep Books are written by Reading Recovery® teachers and other early literacy specialists who know leveled books well. They are called Keep Books because they are so inexpensive teachers can allow students to take them home. The books from Townsend Press are also sold at a per-book price far below other publishers.

If you are looking for protagonists that are diverse, and for authors, too, that are diverse . . .

One of the most challenging tasks that we faced when curating the Classroom Libraries was finding books that not only serve as perfect supports for readers, but that also have authors and characters who reflect the diversity of readers. While most publishers depict characters from different backgrounds, several have adopted diversity as a core part of their mission. If you are seeking fiction that highlights diverse characters, you will want to check out Lee & Low's collection of Bebop Leveled Readers and also seek out read-alouds from Lee & Low's higher-level options. Another publisher that specializes in leveled fiction with diverse characters is Townsend Press, and we are especially enthusiastic about their King School series, which includes stories and situations that young readers can relate to, thus positioning readers to engage in deeper thinking and conversations around these texts. You can also find diverse characters in Capstone's early chapter book series—all of which we love. You'll see we have included titles from the Katie Woo and Sofia Martinez series in the libraries.

If you are looking for books that support your content-area instruction . . .

You may also want to build out your library to include books on specific topics covered in your school's curriculum. Sundance/Newbridge publishes more than 3,000 nonfiction books leveled across grades K–8, and their collection represents a wide range of topics, from gardening to ancient history. These well-structured texts are a great starting place on content-area topics that will engage students. You can purchase many texts from Newbridge as big books, and they also offer small copies of these texts.

If you are looking for series books at transitional levels . . .

When readers are transitioning into early chapter books, we want them to begin reading many of the popular early chapter books and series from larger trade book publishers—Henry and Mudge, Iris and Walter, Frog and Toad, Houndsley and Catina, Mercy Watson, Pinky and Rex, The Princess in Black, Horrible Harry, Poppleton, and so on. These readers are at an exciting turning point in their reading life. They aren't just reading longer books, they are reading chapter books—the books they have seen their older siblings and friends reading and talking about.

Some of these texts are episodic (each chapter is a different story/adventure), and some are cumulative. In either case, readers are introduced to characters who go on adventures and encounter problems. These texts set readers up to accumulate longer texts and plotlines, all the while putting themselves in the shoes of the characters, thinking about their relationships and the lessons learned.

You can find series books at the trade publishers—for example, Simon and Schuster publishes Henry and Mudge, Harcourt Children's Books publishes Iris and Walter; HarperCollins publishes Frog and Toad; Candlewick is famous especially for Houndsley and Catina, Mercy Watson, and The Princess in Black; Simon Spotlight is the place to find Pinky and Rex; Puffin Books provides us with Horrible Harry; and Blue Sky Press is the source of the Poppleton series. There are, of course, still other wonderful series and other places to find those series.

If You're Looking For . . .	Try (among other places) . . .
Well-leveled, highly supportive text across a wide range of levels	• Hameray • Rigby • Sunshine Books New Zealand

Engaging and beautiful, high-interest nonfiction	• Discovery Kids Readers
	• Pioneer Valley
	   Explore the World series
	   Discover Our World series
	• Riverstream
	• Sundance/Newbridge
	   Discovery Links series
	   Early Science series

Great fiction for shared reading	• Hameray • Richard C. Owen • Rigby

Character series for beginning readers	• Candlewick Press
	   Brand New Readers series
	• Kaeden Books
	   Fishing series
	   Sammy series
	• Pioneer Valley
	   Quack the Duck series
	   Bella and Rosie series
	   Jasper the Cat series
	   Gilbert the Pig series
	• Townsend Press
	   King School series

Fiction with characters from diverse backgrounds	• Capstone • Kaeden • Lee & Low • Townsend Press *King School series*
Great fiction at low levels	• Blueberry Hill • Flying Start • Kaeden • MaryRuth • Rigby
High-quality illustrations that match the words in the text to support the reader	• Kaeden • Richard C. Owen
Well-written books on a tight budget	• Candlewick *Brand New Readers series* • Keep Books • Townsend Press

Chapter 5

The Process of Building the Leveled Book Shelves

The leveled book shelves are at the heart of the K–2 TCRWP Classroom Libraries. Before we could select books for those shelves, however, we needed to review all of the candidate books to determine their reading level. Books often came to us with levels assigned, but those levels came from a host of different sources, and there were great inconsistencies between how those different places derived their levels. We therefore assembled a team of people with deep expertise in leveling K–2 books, and began the great work of leveling.

In the end, many reviewers read and carefully reconsidered the assigned levels (if there had been any) on each book that was considered for inclusion in one of the libraries when we were confident that our levels would be more accurate. The only levels we did not adjust were those set by Fountas and Pinnell, whose levels we trust.

In doing this work, we began by calling to mind a few readers at the particular level under consideration. Then we thought about the details of the work that those readers could do and could *almost* do. Then, informed by that clear understanding of the readers we had in mind, we chose books that we knew would give the students we had in mind rich opportunities to carry out the work they needed opportunities to be doing.

It was a mammoth undertaking. But the end result is a library that will not only be special for kids, but will also be special for you.

The Important Preliminaries: The Right Expertise, the Right System, and a Mountain of Books

Relying on the Judgment of Both Teachers and Experts

Leveling books in a classroom library has always been an enormous undertaking. Countless primary teachers have stayed late in their classrooms to level a mountain

of books, sorting each into the appropriate bin, and affixing a colored dot to each book's cover. In recent years, some companies have developed leveling equations designed to take the need for teacher judgment out of this process, replacing that judgment with a tool or a formula that does the job of leveling the classroom library. Oftentimes this is done by isolating a particular text characteristic—such as the length of sentences across the entire text, or the average number of syllables per word. This is one (flawed) way to get libraries leveled in short order.

We prefer to take into account multiple factors, which in the end also means relying on expert judgment. We recruited Joe Yukish, former Senior Reading Specialist at the TCRWP and before that, a trainer of the trainers with Reading Recovery, to help us level and relevel all the books. We also brought in TCRWP staff developers and others who have special expertise in that work.

Choosing a Leveling System: Fountas and Pinnell

As mentioned earlier, most of the books we reviewed arrived with some evidence of having been leveled using one system or another. One bore the label Book 2, one was called Easy Reader, a third was part of a line of books called Swing into Reading. We set out to translate all those varied codes into a single cohesive leveling system, so that we could then slot the books into the right bin, then choose the very best of those books. We decided to level according to the Fountas and Pinnell (2006) leveling system, which assigns texts into one of twenty-six (A–Z) levels of text difficulty. When you compare books that have been leveled by Fountas and Pinnell to those that have been leveled using other systems, you will see that the factors predominant in other systems (sentence complexity/length, decodability of words) are taken into account in the F&P system, but the F&P system takes other factors into account as well.

Gathering Books for Consideration

Our first job was to receive whatever book recommendations we could and then to locate as many fabulous publishers of K–2 books as possible, and to study their lines of books. Each expert in primary literacy touted his or her own somewhat small list of favorite publishers. It was crucial to pool knowledge, to study websites and other sources, and also to attend national conferences. Through this system, we developed our knowledge base of publishers who produce books for emergent and beginning readers, and secured books from each of those publishers.

This was an iterative process because we first studied the offerings at a publisher, then homed in on what we saw as the strengths of that publisher, and then of course needed to examine every book in that area of strength.

Organizing and Reviewing the Books by Level

Before we could read through the books and decide whether they merited further consideration based on their information, their storylines, and their quality, we needed to divide our mountains of books according to levels using Fountas and Pinnell's leveled book database. For example, we had a mountain of level C books, so we asked, "Is this book *really* requiring readers to do the work of level C? Is the content of the story realistic?" If the book was nonfiction, we asked, "Are the demands of a nonfiction text within the experiential background of a level C reader?" These questions became essential for us and were repeated at every level, guided by the descriptions of the work required at each level. When you add books to the leveled bins in your classroom library, you may be able to use this same system to double-check the levels of those new books.

Understanding the Work of the Level

We began by picturing a level C reader. This is a child who can point accurately to each word as she reads it. When a word changes in the repeated sentences (I see a *lion* at the zoo/I see a *bear* at the zoo) this reader can draw on the repeated words in the repetitive language pattern, the content of the story (i.e., zoo animals), and the illustration to help her read the one word that has changed. As she moves into level C, she must begin to use known sight words and initial letter sounds to figure out words that are not supported in the illustration. Some students may be confused about the name of zoo animals, calling a lion a tiger. When they use the sound of the first letter /l/, the word has to be *lion*. Another demand of level C is that the reader must also recognize and understand a wider array of high-frequency words while still working in a repetitive structure.

These challenges are illustrated in Jenny Giles's *My Book*. To read, "I am looking for my book. / My book is not here. / Look! / Here is my elephant," the reader must know and recognize several sight words (*I, am, is, my, here, look*) and know to check the picture, depicting a bookshelf, with the initial sound of the letter /b/ to word solve *book*. As she continues, she will rely on combining this pattern with her knowledge of sight words to detect a pattern change. "I am looking for my book. / My book is not *up* here. / Look! / Here is my *monkey*." As she reads, she must recognize that a word has been added to the sentence structure and that that word is the familiar sight word *up*. This is the work of level C.

As we sorted through, we sought out books that would allow the reader to practice recognizing sight words and using the first letter to solve unfamiliar words by thinking about what was going on in the story and searching for information in the illustration. In the example, "I am looking for my book. / My book is not up here. / Look! / Here is my *monkey*," our reader must read the sentence, realizing the target word is *monkey* and not *toy*.

Setting Aside Books that Require Work beyond Level

To keep our readers focused on this work, we eliminated books that had been leveled as C books but that asked students to take on work beyond the limits of this level. For example, books with initial blends and limited picture support were moved to level D, where initial blends are first introduced. It wouldn't be fair to ask a student reading on level C to word solve *closet* from the blend /cl/ or *dresser* from the blend /dr/ without exceptionally clear picture support and without being sure the word is in the student's spoken vocabulary. We eliminated other books because they contained contractions or other words that required decoding skills not yet mastered by a reader on this level. By eliminating books with these overly challenging aspects, we allow our level C reader to move quickly through the level, fully mastering searching for and using initial consonants, and setting her up for the work with initial blends and a wider range of sight words she will encounter in level D.

Creating a Spectrum of Difficulties within the Level

Within this level and every level, we worked to create a spectrum of difficulties, highlighting the important aspects of text complexity. For example, some books within level C will ask students to tackle assigned dialogue, while others will have students navigating more complex and frequent pattern changes or increased levels of book language. Across all of these books, they will continue the big work of searching for and using meaning from what is happening in the story and pictures, as well as automatic sight word recognition.

Organizing and Reviewing the Books by Level: Increasing Text Complexity

Continuing this process across the levels, we found that as levels increase, so do the number of aspects of text complexity that must be considered when developing a collection of books at that level. For example, when working on level K, we again imagined a reader at this level. He can no longer rely on picture support as he reads and must read through longer stretches, making a movie in his mind as he reads. (At the beginning levels of reading (A–J), teaching children to attend to illustrations and how they support meaning helps them use the visual images to create "a movie in their mind" when illustrations no longer appear on each page of a story.) A level K reader knows how to track a typical story structure and works to accumulate text over longer stories with multiple plot episodes. He also begins to track multiple characters throughout a story and compares each character to people he knows in real life. This level K reader is far more independent and has begun to develop clear reading preferences.

As we considered books for the level K fiction shelves, we imagined the different types of texts that might support our level K reader: series books, little leveled books, and commercial picture books.

Allington (2012b) notes that simplification is created in series books by repeated proper nouns and known characters, allowing readers to build volume as they more comfortably accumulate stories over longer texts. This will ultimately allow a reader access to more challenging and higher-quality literature. A reader who began to read across a series on level I and is now moving into K will find that the experience of being a series reader will continue to lift the level of his thinking. He will track longer plotlines by envisioning and tracking the events of the story, as well as noticing characters' actions and dialogue. All of this blends together, allowing our reader to draw conclusions about who characters are and why they do the things they do. What's more, he'll discover characters he loves who will carry him across many more books.

As he reads across a series, our level K reader must begin to understand that characters have multiple traits. For example, in a series book like *Houndsley and Catina*, our reader learns that Catina wants to be a writer, is a vegetarian, and has a best friend named Houndsley, all within the first ten pages of the story. Fiction books at this level must support this kind of thinking as the reader puts together multiple pieces of information to better understand his characters as multifaceted beings.

Not all books across this level will fall into the early chapter book series category, however. Smaller leveled books compose a surprisingly meaty aspect of the level K shelf. Books such as Gare Thompson's retelling of *The Lion and the Mouse* are shorter, but still play an important role in helping readers achieve the work of level K that contains a higher number of multisyllable or irregular words that are more difficult to decode and a higher ratio of thoughts per word.

While our reader worked to accumulate facts about characters in *Houndsley and Catina*, he dives deeply into more complex and developed characters and plot in *The Lion and the Mouse*. He will encounter aspects of fable, increasing his knowledge about genre, and about what the characters do and why they do it. Additionally, by identifying the lessons learned within short texts, the reader can begin the work of moving from literal thinking to delving into larger life lessons about big ideas, such as friendship and courage. The potential for rereading is high, and these little books can powerfully alter the way readers see the world around them.

Commercially available picture books compose an important aspect of the leveled book shelves above level I. While these books adhere less strictly to the work of the level, books such as Mem Fox's *Koala Lou* help to foster a deep love of reading with silly plots and compelling illustrations. For more flexible and proficient readers, such books increase repertoire while also making for lively, engaging read-alouds that children will love.

Within the level K bins, you will find a balance of books from these categories, representing the increased repertoire of a reader at this transitional level. This range of options keeps reading interesting, allowing children to seek out characters and genres they love that will carry them on their journey of lifelong reading.

We approached nonfiction with a similarly critical eye, seeking out a range of interesting topics presented in level-supportive texts. At level K, nonfiction

becomes more complex as readers begin learning more technical language from their texts. Readers also begin to navigate headings and sections within the larger topic of the text. For example, while reading Sarah O'Neil's *Volcanoes*, our reader will find different types of information under the heading "Lava and Ash" than he will under the heading "Where Volcanoes Are Found." Within the text, he will encounter domain-specific vocabulary alongside its definition. For example, he will read, "Volcanoes that haven't erupted for a long time are called *dormant*." With the definition available on the spot, not requiring the reader to use a dictionary or glossary, he can immediately add the word *dormant* to the technical vocabulary he knows about volcanoes.

As with the earlier levels, we set aside books that purported to be at level K but that fell so far outside our reader's abilities that the book would not help the reader grow. For example, some books asked our reader to navigate unfamiliar content vocabulary without providing a definition for the targeted words within the text. Initially readers need to be taught the vocabulary in the text to realize the value of mastering those words in bold print or other words that are not in their vocabulary. Eventually they will be expected to do this work on their own using other devices. According to the leveling system we are using, a reader should not be expected to rely on a glossary until he reaches level N. With this in mind, we employed a rule of three strikes and you're out. Our reader might be able to guess at one or two unfamiliar words without detracting from comprehension; however, the eventual tipping point comes when such unfamiliar words recur throughout a text. One such book, although of incredibly high interest, demanded readers navigate baseball content words such as *pennant, exhibition,* and *memorabilia.* That book, however, provided no text or picture support for these terms, raising the level of the text far beyond what we could expect of our level K reader.

Selecting Texts to Exemplify the Work of a Level

As we continued to grow out each leveled book shelf, we kept these benchmark students in mind. We also selected prototypical texts such as *My Book, Volcanoes,* and *Houndsley and Catina* that exemplified the variety of work to be done within a given level. These texts serve as the cornerstone of each leveled book shelf and provide a solid foundation upon which to build. These texts can continue to guide you as you grow and expand the collection in your own classroom.

Worth noting as well is that each text is not a perfect 100% fit for each level. Just as eating only one food, however nutritious, will not make our bodies grow, reading only one type of book will not help our readers grow strong reading skills. The collection as a whole needs to boost readers, allowing them to do different types of work, just as *Houndsley and Catina* and *Volcanoes* helped our level K reader work on different skills across the level. Each level represents a range of different reading skills for students to build on. For example, in a level C basket not every book must have tagged dialogue, but enough should include books with tagged dialogue that students can master that aspect of the level. Readers need a diet of different types of book that provide them with different challenges. If each book met a level's criteria too closely, they would all read in the exact same way, creating an inauthentic representation of what literature actually looks like.

Using Our Process as a Model

The TCRWP Classroom Libraries and the process for creating them can become a model for you to expand each level of your library with more books. The key thing to keep in mind is that with leveled books for K–2 readers, it's not just *the author* that matters, but *the publishers* as well. (In Chapter 4, we shared some of the behind-the-scenes scoop we've enjoyed learning about these publishers.)

Chances are good that when you first began collecting books for your own classroom library, you drew on books from just a handful of publishers that produce books for early readers. Each of those publishers has its own trademark ways that books are written, and many rely on the same author and use the same formula for a great many of their books. These TCRWP Classroom Libraries access well over twenty publishers' books for young readers; many of these may be new to you and enable you to expand your list of trustworthy sources for great K–2 books.

A team of Teachers College Reading and Writing Project staff developers, Reading Recovery teacher-leaders, and graduate students worked for months to select the books that you now see within each leveled bin. The work we did is work you will want to approximate when you expand your library. But always, as you continue to develop and grow your library, remember that levels provide a strong framework, but that too rigid an adherence to a leveled library might cause readers to miss out on great books that will help them grow.

Chapter 6

Assessing Students and Matching Readers to Books

Before you can match texts to your students that are within reach for them, you'll need to conduct assessments to determine where they are as readers. For each child, you'll want to find out how she processes text, how much she understands what she is reading, and what kind of thinking work she is doing. The more you know about your readers, the more wisely you can teach them, the more strategic the partnerships you set up will be, and the more informed your conferring and small-group work will be. Reading can feel like invisible work, but with smart assessments, you *can* know what's really going on with your readers.

For emergent readers, children who are not yet reading conventionally, you'll want to find out what they already know about how books work, as well as what each child knows about stories and storytelling. A scale of emergent reading stages will help you know where children stand regarding their ability to tell a story across the pages of a familiar book.

Once your students are beginning to read leveled books, or are beginning to make attempts at conventional writing, you'll want to learn what they know about foundational skills, especially letter-sound identification, spelling patterns, and high-frequency words. You'll also want to use running records to learn how each child is processing text.

Assessing Readers Using Fountas and Pinnell's Leveling System

As mentioned in Chapter 5, the reading levels we use in the Classroom Libraries come from Irene Fountas and Gay Su Pinnell's work wherever possible. The reading levels span from A to Z+ and represent a gradient of ways that books become more complex, from a very beginning level to adult texts. For more information on reading levels, you might read *Leveled Books, K–8: Matching Texts to Readers for Effective Teaching* by Irene Fountas and Gay Su Pinnell (Heinemann 2005).

The leveling system will only be truly useful if you also use running records to determine the level of text complexity that your readers can just handle. There are a variety of materials available that support teachers in conducting running records. Fountas and Pinnell have produced a boxed Benchmark Assessment system. Alternatively, your school may have versions of the DRA or the QRI. The Teachers College Reading and Writing Project offers a free download of running records; you can learn more about those at our website (readingandwritingproject. org). The tools on the TCRWP website aren't better; they're just shorter and free of charge. In the end, all of these systems essentially accomplish the same task.

When conducting running records, you'll ask a child to read up a ladder of increasingly difficult texts. Within a few minutes, you get a snapshot of a child's fluency, accuracy, and literal inferential comprehension with texts on a particular level of text complexity. You can then track how these change as the youngster tackles progressively more challenging texts. This assessment tool provides a window into what's happening in a child's mind—information that can guide your teaching decisions and help you and your children know how they are progressing as readers.

Some may critique these assessments as reductive—and of course, describing a reader by identifying the level of text difficulty that the child can independently handle is not a sufficiently rich description of that child's reading. But as one component of a system of reading assessment and instruction, it does provide schools, teachers, and caregivers a leg up as they work to identify needs and ensure success for each student.

You will want to assess other ways in which youngsters grow as readers, because running records do not provide information about a child's fluency, or a child's ability to read critically, interpret, compare and contrast, or do a lot of other important skill work. If you teach with Units of Study for Teaching Reading, you will find performance assessments that give a great deal more information and help you keep your eye on a child's higher-level comprehension.

To use running records effectively, we believe it is essential that you norm the way teachers across your school assess running records. A quick introductory course on giving running records is also helpful. Many small decisions are made when conducting a running record: What percentage of comprehension questions must be answered correctly to pass? Is a repeated miscue counted once or every time? Taken together, these judgments can have an enormous impact not only on the progress students make class-wide, but also on their trajectory as they move through grades.

A Book's Level of Text Complexity Suggests the Work Its Readers Need to Do

Your knowledge of levels of text complexity and of a particular book's "level" will be very helpful as you work with students. Even if you do not know a particular book, chances are good that you'll know the specific kinds of work the text will ask a reader to do—just from your knowledge of the text level.

So if you pull your chair alongside a child who is reading a level I book, for example, you draw on your knowledge of text complexity to be able to say something like, "I know that in many books at this level, readers keep on getting to know more about the characters as they read on. Can you walk me through what you knew early on about the characters in this story? And then can you tell me some newer things you've been learning about the book's characters as you read?"

What kind of work is called for in level A?

Books at this level assist children in looking at print and matching the words that they read with the words on the page. That is, the child learns to say one word as she points to one word. Often the child knows what the page says because the text is patterned. The words are supported by the picture, so the reader's job is a one-to-one match. Books at this level allow a teacher to observe if a student knows how to "look at" and "move through" print; the objective of decoding text begins at higher levels. Level A books are highly predictable, and children benefit from using the title and the cover of the book to get the "big idea" of what the book will be about. In most cases the pattern on the first page will be repeated throughout the book. This provides enough support so that the child can do the job of matching her spoken words to the written ones. The text is most often comprised of one-syllable words to avoid added difficulty with one-to-one matching. If there is a multisyllabic word, it's usually at the end of a sentence.

Cat and Mouse, *by Phyllis Root, Brand New Readers*

What kind of work is called for in level B?

Books at this level continue to assist children in one-to-one matching of the words that they read with the words on the page. The student is still not required to decode text using letter-sound relationships; the child doesn't yet look at the first letters of a word to decide what it says, but instead looks at the picture and thinks about what the book is about.

Level B books continue to be highly predictable, and the pattern goes a long way to helping the child read. The title and the cover picture help the reader get the "big idea" of what the book is about, and that is important because the child doesn't rely on pattern alone to read level B books. The pattern on the first page is usually repeated throughout the book until the end, which often has a slight pattern change. Readers are helped with this, because usually when a sentence breaks the pattern, the first word in that sentence—the first hint that the pattern has changed—is a known high-frequency word.

The other big change that readers encounter when moving to level B books is that now there are two and sometimes three lines of text per page, requiring the student to make a return sweep to the beginning of the next line. In addition, words with more than one syllable often occur in the middle of a sentence. This requires the reader to hold his finger on the word until he says the whole word. If not, the presence of two-syllable words can knock one-to-one matching awry. It is more critical than ever to make sure the student is pointing under the words at this level and also using the words he knows as anchor words to lock in his matching.

What kind of work is called for in level C?

In level C books, readers need to rely on a growing knowledge of letters and sounds—graphophonics. The pictures are less supportive; the same picture could yield any of a few different words. For example, in *Can you see the eggs?*, one sentence says, "Mother Blackbird is in the tree." The picture shows the bird perched in some sort of plant, so the reader must decide if the last word is *bush*, *tree*, or *plant*. The picture helps the reader know that one of these words is likely correct, but the reader must decide on the word *tree* by recognizing the /t/ beginning.

That book is also a good example of ways in which the formatting of texts at level C becomes more complex. The words will not always be in the same place on a page.

At this stage, a reader's pointing shifts so that she points *under* the word and at times, points under the beginning letter, to focus her attention on the important grap-

Can you see the eggs?, *PM Platinum*

hophonic/visual features in the word (usually this is the first letter). Sentences in level C books are longer, and the child's growing bank of known words helps her move across those longer sentences with more ease, able to think about the meaning and the beginning sounds.

The new focus on letters can't come at the cost of a continued focus on meaning, which for kids translates into a focus on the story, the pictures, and the topic.

What kind of work is called for in level D?

Level D books require a reader to look at the letters at the beginnings and the endings of words, using the sounds those letters make to check that he has read the word correctly. For example, in *Swimming with Mermaids* by Michèle Dufresne, Clarence the dragon is trying to get his friend Lily to join him for a swim. As Clarence calls Lily to come in the water, she responds, "The waves are too big." If the reader looked only at the first letter of *waves*, he might say the word *water*. However, the reader who looks at the beginning and the end of the word will see that the word does not end in /r/, which would be necessary for it to say *water*. Through this process the reader settles on the word, saying *waves*.

"No!" said Lily.
"The waves are too big."

Swimming with Mermaids, *by Michèle Dufresne*

Some might ask, "Why not expect students to look at more letters in words beyond the beginning and ending letters?" That expectation becomes real at higher levels, but remember, these early levels A, B, C, and D are designed to make children comfortable looking at and moving through print, applying their beginning letter-sound knowledge. The start or end of a word may contain a consonant blend or a digraph. Readers of level C and D books are in the rudimentary alphabetic stage of reading development, knowing most letters and their sounds, and attending to beginning and endings in words.

The books in level D continue to have a pattern, but the pattern may be different on the first page and on the last page, so that it is just the internal part of the book that maintains the same pattern.

When you are teaching readers who are working with level D books, you will want to assess whether your students know the sounds for consonant blends (i.e., *br, cl*, etc.) and for digraphs (*sh, ch*, etc.). This is also a time to teach readers some common inflectional endings (*-s, -es, -ing, -ed*).

What kind of work is called for in level E?

The illustrations in level E books are less supportive, the sentences are more complex, and the patterns in the books shift part way through them. Children reading these books need to draw on many sources of information, including the text's meaning and the syntax (or sound of the sentence, the kind of word this must be).

Readers of these books not only check beginnings and endings of words, they also look all the way across words, noticing the internal letters. A good way to teach this is to have children check the consonant letter(s) at the start of a word, plus the next two letters. For example, in *Ollie the Stomper* by Olivier Dunrea, a young reader who is stuck on the word *boots* could check the (b+oo). The /oo/ sound will be familiar from known words, such as *too* or *moo*, and the /b/ will get the student to read /boo/. The reader can then use

Ollie stares at his boots.

"These boots are too hot!"
Ollie shouts.

28   29

Ollie the Stomper, *by Olivier Dunrea*

what they know from the story and pictures to find a word that makes sense: *boots*. The reader will then return to the word and check to make sure the letters match up with the word he has said.

Even when a child can say the words in books at this level, there can still be more challenges. Level E books contain more literary language and unusual language structures, as well as more dialogue.

Emma came to the sandbox.
She looked at
Sally and Rebecca
having fun.

Sally's Friends, by Beverley Randell

What kind of work is called for in level F?

Level F books often contain several episodes, which the reader needs to keep in mind and blend together into a coherent storyline. Characters are more developed, and readers are expected to draw inferences about characters. For example, in *Sally's Friends* by Beverley Randell, readers must infer why Sally decides to let Emma play with her, despite her earlier rudeness.

The language in these texts is also more challenging. There is far less repetition in sentences. The literary language that began to show up in level E is even more prevalent. Level F books often include long dialogue that is broken up in the middle by a dialogue tag that assigns the speaker. Readers learn about what characters are doing, how they do it, and where they do it, and this leads to sentences that are syntactically longer and more complex, often containing embedded prepositional phrases and adjectives. In word work, students must continue to deal with irregular spelling patterns (*-ight* in *right*), inflectional endings, plurals, contractions, and possessives.

What kind of work is called for in level G?

Level G books expose students to a wider range of texts, including simple animal fantasy, realistic fiction,

Rosie looked at the little puppy.
Then she looked at the books.
The puppy was chewing on some books!
"Oh, no," said Rosie.
"Look at this mess!
Bad puppy! Mom will be mad!"

Puppy Trouble, by Michèle Dufresne

and folktales. These books require children to integrate all sources of information while reading to understand the author's story or message. There is minimal repetition of familiar sentence patterns, requiring children to attend to more complex story patterns with more difficult vocabulary and story elements. The books have three to eight lines of print on the page, but size of font is now decreasing.

Readers who can handle this level are now automatic with their early reading behaviors, so their attention can focus on the new challenging parts that include more complex vocabulary and words with irregular spelling patterns. To word solve, students should be independently using the strategy taught in earlier levels of using parts of known words to solve unknown words. While keeping meaning in mind, they should be applying phonics rules with the understanding that there are irregular words that don't conform to these rules.

Fluency is important for readers at this level. Readers should aim to read in phrases while beginning to use bold print or punctuation marks to read with intonation and expression.

I'm too tall, *by Barbara Stavetski*

What kind of work is called for in level H?

Books at this level contain more complex literary (story) language, more complex vocabulary, and often more technical vocabulary, especially in informational books. From this level forward, picture support is minimal and requires readers to make clear mental images and connections to their own experiences in life or in other books. In earlier books, episodes were repeated, but in level H there is less repetition of episodes, requiring the student to keep the events of the story in order and relate the events to each other to get the big idea of the story.

Level H books include more dialogue between characters, as well as more elaborate plots and characters. The primary reading work that readers do when reading books at level H revolves around comprehension. Readers at this level also encounter more words with irregular spelling patterns, polysyllabic words with inflectional endings, plurals, contractions, and possessives.

By now, readers need at least a bank of one hundred known high-frequency words, as the knowledge of those words frees readers up to focus on comprehension.

What kind of work is called for in level I?

Books at level I are longer (six to eighteen pages), and some short

The Dinosaur Chase, *by Hugh Price*

chapter books (forty to sixty pages) are introduced at this level. Students must develop skill in attending and accumulating information across a story. Longer, more complex sentences, such as "Then Little Dinosaur raced down to the ferns that grew in the wet mud by the river," in *The Dinosaur Chase*, require the reader to accumulate information across the phrases of a sentence to envision the scene in the story. Level I books often contain more complex literary (story) language, more complex vocabulary, and often more technical vocabulary, especially in informational books. As in level H, the minimal picture support requires readers to use the text to make clear mental images and connections to their own experiences in life or in other books.

Readers who are reading level H and I books tend to find the comprehension more challenging than the word work. Nevertheless, word work continues, as readers will encounter words with irregular spelling patterns, polysyllabic words, and many words with inflectional endings, contractions, and possessives.

What kind of work is called for in level J?

While books at this level J are similar in length and type to level I, students are exposed to new genres at this level: more complex nonfiction, simple biographies, and more complex traditional folktales. As in both levels H and I, picture support is minimal, so readers need to make clear mental images in part by drawing on their own experiences, bringing life-connections to the book. Readers will encounter longer, more complex sentences, such as, "'Hold on, Iris. Hold on tight,' said Walter. 'Whatever you do, don't let go!'" or "'How could I forget?' said her dad" or "There is nothing better than a snowy day."

Some readers of level J books will struggle with decoding. Readers will encounter words with many syllables that also have inflectional endings, suffixes, prefixes, plurals, contractions, and possessives. Being able to process these words quickly and effectively frees the reader's processing to focus on comprehension and fluent reading.

Iris and Walter: True Friends, *by Elissa Haden Guest*

What kind of work is called for in level K and beyond?

In level K and beyond, children are reading early chapter books. At these higher levels, the books are longer and divided into chapters, and the role of rereading changes significantly. Children no longer read a book, then reread it, then reread it once more. Instead, children will likely reread only if you encourage them to do so. You can suggest that readers choose especially favorite books to reread to find more in them to appreciate. When you push readers to have ideas about what

Tomorrow

Toad woke up.

"Drat!" he said.

"This house is a mess.

I have so much work to do."

Frog looked through the window.

"Toad, you are right,"

said Frog. "It is a mess."

Toad pulled the covers

over his head.

4

"I will do it tomorrow,"

said Toad.

"Today I will take life easy."

5

Days with Frog and Toad, *by Arnold Lobel*

they're reading, you can help them reflect not just on the sequence of events (which is what they're apt to be preoccupied with), but also on a character's wants, or the relationships between characters, or the cause-and-effect relationships between events.

Readers at level K and beyond face a number of challenges:

- There is a greater variety of genres, including mystery, simple fantasy, fairy tales and folk-tales, myths, legends, and biographies.

- Illustrations gradually disappear. They provide a backdrop for the story in level J but are almost nonexistent in level M books.

- Children need to use what they know about story structure and elements to help them track longer, more complex stories.

- Character work becomes increasingly more difficult. Students keep track of many characters, accumulate traits explicitly stated in the text, and think about relationships. As readers move to level M, the traits become less explicit and the reader has to do more inferential work to figure out what the character is like.

- Nonfiction texts become more complex, with more technical language explained in the text, and information is divided in sections by boldface headings and content.

- Sentences are longer and contain information embedded in more complex structures.

- Readers must grapple with unfamiliar vocabulary and figurative language, and they must develop strategies for understanding what these words and phrases mean.

- Phonological and phonics skills must be well developed, because words with irregular sound patterns are more common. Polysyllabic words require going across the word by word part or chunk.

- In essence, word work must be strong to allow for greater attention to comprehension of more complex text.

Helping Students Choose Just-Right Texts

At the beginning of kindergarten, most of your students will not yet be reading conventionally, and will not yet be "shopping" for leveled books from bins in your classroom. These students will be developing concepts of print and acquainting themselves with the elements of story. Your assessment of these readers will focus on their work with emergent storybooks, rich storybooks they have heard several times. To match preconventional readers to texts, you will want to select high-interest fiction with predictable plotlines and supportive illustrations, as well as high-interest nonfiction with vivid photographs and familiar concepts for your youngsters to explore.

For students who are reading conventionally and are relatively new to independent reading and choosing just-right books, you will want to teach a minilesson early in the year about how to select books that are just right. To do this, you could pull out a little stack of books and demonstrate how you choose a book that is just right. Perhaps the first book you pull out from the pile is too easy, the kind of book you would have read years before. "This book is probably too easy for me," you might say. "It's the kind of book I might read on vacation as a beach read, but I'm not sure it will help me get stronger as a reader."

Next, you might pull out a thicker book and dramatize how you struggle through it, reading a bit aloud and miscuing on several words on the first page as you read. "Whew, this book is just *too hard*," you might say, "because I don't have *a clue* what's going on here. I'll have to save this one for later." Finally, you might pull out a within-reach book and show students how you determine that this book is just right: it's one you can read smoothly, without many miscues on the page; it's one you understand well; and it's one you are interested in reading. Then, you could rally students to try the same thing, reading a chunk of a text and working to determine whether it's too easy, too hard, or within reach.

You might choose to use some of your one-on-one time with students to ensure they're matched well with books. Ask a child to read aloud a little of his book to you, then pause him and say, "Can you tell me a bit about what's happening in your book so far?" If the child has more than three miscues on the page or has trouble retelling the book, you might look to match that child with a more accessible text. Or, if you notice a child seems disengaged with a text, you might bring him over to the library and share three or four books or series you think might interest him. Your crafty salesmanship can really help get kids excited about a book!

How can I streamline assessment at the beginning of the year?

Many schools find it is enormously helpful if, at the end of a school year, every teacher creates a baggie of books that travels with a child to the child's next grade. The year-ending classroom teacher works with the child to fill the baggie with an old favorite or two and with a batch of new books that promise to be just right or easy (remembering that for children who do not read during the summer, there is always a slide backward) and as enticing as possible. This system allows a teacher who is assessing her incoming class in September to watch those kids working

with books that her colleague believed would be just right. Meanwhile, this process allows this teacher's running records to be informed by a colleague's informal observations. More importantly, it means that every child can get started right away reading books that have been carefully selected for him or her.

Once you have your new class and the children are reading texts that are roughly right for them, you can eyeball to see if youngsters are actually able to read those levels. Did they slip over the summer? If so, it may take just a very short while to get summer rust worn off and to be back to the levels at which they left off.

Professionals other than the classroom teacher can participate in conducting running records and matching readers to books. Many schools hire a reading specialist or others with special training in reading assessment to work with children during summer school or during the final two weeks of summer, conducting assessments and matching books to children. Some schools ask that these professionals conduct all the assessments for those who are particularly at risk, thereby making it likely that these youngsters' time will be maximized, with every moment spent doing work that has been tailored to the child. Other times, schools ask that summer assessments be given to a random sampling of children from every classroom, because having a few already-assessed children dotting a teacher's roster provides another way for classroom teachers to align their assessments with a schoolwide standard. At the very start of the year, some of the school's other specialist teachers may not yet have their "specials" in place, so they might also be asked to help assess readers.

I also recommend that you and all your colleagues become accustomed to assessing students in groups, instead of one-by-one. Bring a cluster of children to the area in which you do assessments, then explain what you'll be doing just once to that whole cluster, asking them to sit near you and start their independent reading while you assess one child after another. You'll find that bringing a group of children together to hear how the running records will go increases the efficiency of your running records.

In the first weeks of school, the priority during your reading assessments is to help each child get access to a book—a stack of books really—that she can read. This is not the time to dive into conducting any one assessment in depth, discovering every detail of that reader's strengths, preferences, and needs. For now, it is more critical that you buzz through the whole class, conducting quick assessments that allow you to launch all students into reading just-right books—and, better yet, reading with a partner who is working at about the same text level. If you get every child roughly assessed within the first two weeks of the school year, there will be time later to conduct more detailed, rigorous assessments and to follow up on all the questions that your initial assessments provoke.

What do running records look like across the year?

Your school will probably also want to establish that teachers conduct semi-formal running records at regular intervals across the year. As mentioned earlier, most of the schools with which we work give running records at predetermined times, at least four times a year, for all readers (RTI requires five) and much more often for lower-level readers and children who read below grade level. Formal windows for conducting running records are quite common and have their advantages, but they also are problematic, because it is common for teachers to only assess during those windows, and children often need to progress to new levels far more often. For example, assuming you assess at the start of the year, you'll find that within a month, the summer rust will have worn off for many readers, and they'll be able to progress to higher levels. It is imperative, then, that assessing readers becomes no big deal.

Assessing Is About Far More Than Establishing the Level of Text Difficulty a Reader Can Handle

Your first job at the start of the year is to fall in love with each and every student—right away. That is not always easy when you are still mourning the loss of last year's kids—and when you have multiple sections of students to get to know.

At the start of the year, I recommend that you find ways—straight away—to invite students to teach you who they are and what they care about as people and as readers and writers. During those first days of the school year, when no one is yet accustomed to sitting at a desk all day anyhow, it is important to set children up to represent their strengths, interests, quirks, and habits as readers and writers. Perhaps you'll give each child a square of the bulletin board, and ask each one to bring in stuff that shows what they like to do as readers. That's a more powerful idea than you might think. Imagine if you were asked to fill a square of the bulletin board with things that show *you* as a reader. Which books, of all that you have ever read in your whole life, would you choose to put into that square? What ways of responding to reading would go there? It's not lightweight work to take the time to construct images of who we are as readers and to put those out into the world.

All of this work will allow you to begin to develop some language about how each of your readers is different from other readers. To one child, you might say, "You've got this way of reading and asking questions that gets to the heart of everything. It's such a special thing, because your questions take us into deep conversations. I hope over the year, you teach us how you do that." The important thing to realize is that that child might be reading books that are the least complex of any books being read in the class, and yet the child is not just a reader who is working with that level of text. She is also an inquirer and a teacher of inquiry to the class.

The point is that you can temper the emphasis on a ladder-like progression of reading development if you highlight the many ways your students have composed reading lives for themselves. Each student is a complex combination of habits, aspirations, talents, preferences, and worries—far more than just a text level. Once you match kids to books, chances are good there will be talk such as, "I'm a G reader." You'll want to have the goods to broaden and balance that. You might say, "You are also our class expert on pets. You helped us use the fish books to decide which types of fish to get for our class fish tank and used your reading to help us all learn how to take care of them."

You have extraordinary power to make each child feel seen and respected!

Chapter 7

Teaching Methods

1 Reading Aloud

The single most important thing you can do to turn your students into readers is to read aloud to them. Read aloud several times a day—read to greet the day, to learn about trees or butterflies or Mars, to celebrate a birthday or a Monday morning, to fall through the rabbit hole of story. Above all, read aloud to immerse children in the glories of reading.

"Read to them," Cynthia Rylant says. "Take their breath away. Read with the same feeling in your throat as when you first see the ocean after driving hours and hours to get there. Close the final page of the book with the same reverence you feel when you kiss your sleeping child at night."

Read from all the genres on your classroom shelves so that you give children a feel for the variety of voices, styles, and kinds of books there are in the world. Read Mem Fox's *Koala Lou* and share in Koala Lou's longing for her mother's love. Then shift gears and read the laugh-out-loud opening to Michael Ian Black's *A Pig Parade Is a Terrible Idea* or read the pleas that start Karen Orloff's *I Wanna Iguana*. Be sure you also read aloud nonfiction texts such as Seymour Simon's *Superstorms*, a book that is bound to stop you in your tracks as you marvel at the destructive power of nature. With each new book you read, use your voice, your expressions, your gestures, and your responses to model your love of reading.

Choosing Books to Read Aloud

As the year progresses, you will want to think carefully about the texts you choose for each day's read-aloud. It's an important decision! Our selection of read-aloud shelves in the TCRWP Classroom Libraries took days, weeks, even months to curate—and of course you will need to select scores more books. Know that the texts you read can open up new topics and even new disciplines for your class, turning your students into scientists, historians, or anthropologists. The texts you choose can also bring your class together—to laugh together, to be outraged together, to cry together.

As you mull over your choice of books, don't shy away from chapter books. Your kids will probably love it if you read aloud powerful, complicated chapter books such as Kate DiCamillo's *The Miraculous Journey of Edward Tulane* or Ted Hughes's *The Iron Giant*. Lots of second-graders love books by Roald Dahl and Dick King-Smith and even C. S. Lewis's Narnia series. If you make fiction reading a mainstay in your classroom, if you read aloud every day and therefore progress through books in a good clip, by all means turn to books such as these.

Especially if you read aloud some of the longer chapter books, it will be very important for you to keep a watchful eye on your momentum through a book. Kids can stay enthralled with a particular book for two weeks—but not two months. Don't let a book drag on for more than two weeks. When you try to stretch a book across too many days, young children can begin to lose the beginning of the book. Time your lengthier read-alouds, then, for periods of the year when you can read your chapter book aloud consistently, reading at least once a day, day after day.

One way to keep up the pace of your read-aloud is to realize that although yes, it is absolutely important to conduct grand conversations in the wake of a read-aloud, it's also perfectly acceptable to read a chapter or two, then close the book, letting a ring of silence linger. Then you can speak into the silence. "I know you're bursting to talk about everything you just heard, but save your thoughts for today, and tomorrow, after reading time, you'll have a chance to hear each other's ideas."

Keep in mind that your youngsters will probably love some of the shorter chapter books as well as picture books. Try Ursula K. Le Guin's Catwings series, or the old favorite, *My Father's Dragon*, or Elissa Haden Guest's series, Iris and Walter. Try picture books such as Angela Johnson's *The Leaving Morning* or Mem Fox's *Koala Lou*. These can be read aloud in one or two sittings, but they merit discussion that lasts past a single day, so you may want to schedule a second day to revisit, reread, and to talk more deeply. Particularly for beginning readers, it is important to read texts that invite new concepts, vocabulary, and big ideas to surface. For example, *Thank You, Mr. Falker* might only take two or three days to read aloud, but it provides kids opportunities to think about larger issues, marvel at beautiful language, and puzzle through sophisticated vocabulary. You can go back to many of these books again and again, rereading for different purposes and with different lenses.

Be similarly thoughtful when selecting nonfiction for read-aloud. Here too, the work you are doing in read-aloud will mirror the types of thinking you want children doing in their own texts. When you read nonfiction aloud, make sure that you take a bit of time to orient yourself to the text before plunging in. Just as you use your voice to help children follow a story, you will want to use your voice to help your children better understand the meaning and vocabulary in your nonfiction read-aloud. Reading nonfiction aloud will spark curiosity in your readers and help them see how engaging nonfiction can be.

Whether the book you read aloud is a chapter book, a picture book, a nonfiction book, a little leveled book, or anything else, the fact that you have read that text to your children gives them opportunities to apply and extend their comprehension skills to that text, and to do so with support from you and company from classmates. For a child whose independent reading level is below benchmark, the fact that you have read aloud a text means that the youngster has the opportunity to apply and extend his or her high-level comprehension skills while wrestling with a grade-appropriate complex text. For all children, your read-aloud invites intellectual stretching.

② Shared Reading

Establishing a Celebratory Spirit for Shared Reading

If you watch teachers who are especially comfortable with shared reading, you'll quickly see that shared reading can feel like a hootenanny. This is whole-group work at its finest, but its roots are in the intimacy of a father reading with his toddler on his lap. That first father was Don Holdaway, the Australian literacy researcher who developed shared reading in an effort to re-create, in the classroom, the experience of what he referred to as lap-reading.

Since then, shared reading has become a staple in any balanced-literacy primary classroom. Its honored position comes not just from the way shared reading brings a class together around a love of reading, but also from the instructional payoff. Shared reading provides a bridge linking direct instruction, active engagement, and independent reading, and connects the work of reading to students, with students, and by students.

First and foremost, you need an inclusive, celebratory spirit and a sense of intimacy. The goal is for all students to be comfortable participating in shared reading

sessions, so that after a few days rereading a text, a chorus of children's voices overtakes yours. To support that sort of engagement, avoid calling on students to read aloud sections of the text to the class, and instead, invite all students to read the text at once, in unison, saying, "Will you join me in reading this book? Let's read with one voice, saying the words together." You'll learn a lot by watching teachers who do this well and I recommend you visit colleagues who feel that shared reading is the best part of their day. View videos of shared reading as well, including those on the Teachers College Reading and Writing Project website.

Shared reading sessions move quickly. Usually shared reading sessions begin with children joining with you to read a warm-up text, and then teachers usually invite children to join in shared reading of the text that will be the focus of that day's shared reading. All of this happens in a span of ten to fifteen minutes.

It is important to keep these sessions brief—in part because that way, you'll do them often. It's equally important to keep your students' levels of engagement sky-high. You will support that sort of engagement by weaving in a few turn-and-talks, saying to students, "Whoa! That felt important! Turn and tell your partner what just happened," or "Wait a sec. I'm confused, aren't you? What are you wondering? Tell your partner."

After a turn-and-talk interlude, I don't recommend you call on individual students to share their thoughts. Instead, you might say something like, "I heard many of you saying that those darn squirrels found a way to get into the bird feeder, despite Old Man Fookwire's great plan," highlighting quickly what you overheard students sharing with each other. This keeps the focus on students' shared experience with the text, rather than on one child's comprehension or fluency, and allows you to maintain momentum while reading.

Whether you choose to point to words and how you do so will depend on students' reading levels and your goals for your students. For students reading at levels A through D—those who need support with one-to-one matching—you will probably point under each word as you read it, mirroring the work you hope your young readers do when reading independently. Then, as the bulk of your students move to levels E and F, you might move to sliding your finger under the line of words. By levels G through I, you'll likely remove that scaffold, putting your finger next to the start of the line so children have support tracking the line being read. Regardless, what researchers such as Tim Rasinski emphasize as critically important is that students are able to see the text and are encouraged to move their eyes across it as they read together.

As you read, you'll demonstrate fluency for students. Model how the book ought to sound, reading it as you hope students soon will, with words grouped together. This means that you'll read it at a good clip—much faster than you might be tempted to read. You'll find the group develops momentum as they read along fluently with you. Don't let the invitation for the children to join in create the feeling that you need to drag them along, resulting in a word-by-word reading.

Shared reading will give your children the conviction, "Of course I can read!"

Watch for the places where your students can take the lead. Think, "This is a place where I know students will leap in, so I can trail my voice off here and really let them take over."

At the start of the year, you can return to a small set of favorite texts day after day, time after time, until you and your students are at home with the process of shared reading. Then you can extend your use of this powerful teaching method to a wider range of texts. Shared reading will give your children the conviction, "Of course I can read!" It will support their sense of agency and their confidence so that they draw on their growing repertoire of strategies to tackle tricky words, build meaning, and read with greater fluency and expression.

Choosing Texts for Shared Reading

When choosing texts for shared reading, you'll probably choose books that are slightly above the independent reading level of the bulk of your class. Imagine you have a class of first-graders. In September, the benchmark level for first grade is D/E. If most of your students are at this level, you'll need to teach and coach into skills and behaviors that will move them toward F/G books, and therefore you will use shared reading texts at these higher levels. If a larger percentage of your students are below or above benchmark level, you'll need to adjust the level of texts, as well as the skills and behaviors you highlight to match students' specific reading needs.

You'll also want to select warm-up shared reading texts. These can be poems, songs, class charts, or interactive writing you've done together. We suggest you read one of these texts briefly, at the start of a shared reading session, as a way to build fluency and warm students up for the work ahead. Of course, these warm-up texts should also be added to students' book baggies.

You'll need some way to make the text you select accessible to students, so all eyes can gather on one shared copy. You might use a document camera to enlarge and project a text, or copy a selection of the text onto chart paper. If you have multiple copies of your chosen book, be sure to give students access to these after the shared reading sessions, so they can read them independently.

Planning Shared Reading across a Week

There are many ways to plan shared reading across a week, but we recommend a plan in which you read the shared text repeatedly over the course of about five days. By returning to the text over and over, you can show your students the ways in which readers return to a text again and again, each time getting more and more out of the text. With so much practice with foundational skills across the text, your students will learn to transfer these skills to the texts they read independently. Remember, you are not just teaching a text, you are also working on sets of skills that students need to orchestrate and integrate in reading all texts. This plan will help you decide both what to teach and how to teach those skills through shared reading.

On the first day with a new book, you might begin by briefly introducing the book and several important vocabulary words or concepts. It's the perfect time to practice using M-S-V to tackle tricky words. On the second day, you might reread the book, this time with a focus on cross-checking to encourage kids to monitor their own reading and become more self-reliant. On the third day you might focus on word study concepts, choosing activities relevant to the word work students need, such as sight words, short vowel patterns, plurals, and syllables. During the fourth time reading the text, you might focus on the three parts of fluency: parsing, pacing, and using prosodic cues. You can help children read all the way without stopping to figure out words or stumbling over pronunciation, while also working on reading neither too quickly nor too slowly, and using prosodic cues—all the meaning cues an author provides, such as punctuation, italicized print, and bold print. During the final time reading the text, you might rally children to put together everything they've practiced all week to read accurately and fluently.

You might choose a different way to plan for shared reading. You might decide to read a different book each day of the week to show your kids how the reading process works in many different kinds of books, or to get your readers involved in using a repertoire of strategies to make meaning from a text. Also, if you want to expose your children to a variety of text types, a book a day can be more powerful than a book a week.

What is most important is that you support readers with comprehension, accuracy, and fluency while keeping the energy level high, whether you do this across five days using the same text, or on one day because you plan to move to a new text on the next day.

③ Independent Reading

My hunch is if I asked each of you, "What are you really after in the teaching of reading?" you'd answer, "I want my students to become lifelong readers." Sometimes we say these words, not realizing that what we actually mean is, "You can judge my teaching by whether my students initiate reading in their own lives, whether they weave books into their lives with the people they know and the passions they feel." These are not small goals.

One of the oldest, simplest ways to do this is to embrace this belief: to support kids to become lifelong readers, give them access to high-interest books, time to read those books, a rich social life around the books, and explicit instruction in the habits, skills, and strategies of proficient readers.

Provide Students with Time for Reading and Access to High-Interest Books of Their Choice

To make schools into places where youngsters thrive as readers, we need to clear out time and space so children can learn to read by *reading*. This means shoveling out the busy work. Speaking at Teachers College, Richard Allington said, with a twinkle in his eye, "*Crap* is the technical term reserved for all the non-reading and non-writing activities that fill kids' days—the dittos, dioramas, papier-mâché maps—all that chases real reading and real writing out of the school day" (2008). In the classrooms of exemplary teachers, students read and write ten times as much as kids in other classes.

Think of it this way. When you teach reading, you are teaching a skill, like playing the oboe or swimming. The learner learns by practicing that skill, not by listening to someone talk about playing the oboe or swimming. As Grant Wiggins said when he spoke at Teachers College, you don't learn to drive by taking a car apart and studying every tiny screw and cog that goes into the car. You need to practice driving. In the same way, your students need to practice the skill of reading.

A mountain of research supports the notion that teachers who teach reading and writing most successfully are those who provide their students with substantial time for actual reading and writing. Allington reports that exemplary teachers of reading have their students reading and writing for as much as half the school day. In typical classrooms, it is not unusual to find kids reading and writing for as little as 10% of the day.

It is no small goal, then, to give students long stretches of time with books they are able to read. In all too many schools, a ninety-minute "reading block" includes no more than ten or fifteen minutes of actual reading (Allington 2002). Students in the classrooms of more effective teachers read ten times as much as students in classrooms of less effective teachers (Allington and Johnston 2002).

Research also suggests that both quantity and quality of reading material are important. In a study called "Does Practice Make Perfect? Independent Reading Quantity, Quality and Student Achievement" (Topping, Samuels, and Paul 2007), data were collected on 45,670 students in grades 1–12. The results indicated that the combination of reading high-quality books in high quantity led to high academic achievement gains. The books you give to your students matter tremendously; they are among your most powerful tools.

Setting Up Independent Reading: Scheduling, Matching Readers to Books, and Managing

If your goal is to help children compose richly literate lives, then you need to give them time each day to do *just that*. The independent reading workshop is the closest you come to seeing how kids author their own reading lives. In reading workshop, children watch each other swapping books, gossiping about characters, reading favorite passages aloud to friends, or searching for information on a hobby, and they say "I want that for myself." You'll see them reading quietly, underlining, and getting ready to tell others about their thinking. Others may be working on reading slightly more difficult texts, and you'll see them previewing the texts or orienting themselves to the topic. Still others may be working on teaching someone else about all they've learned from a nonfiction book, using the illustrations to highlight their teaching.

> The independent reading workshop is the closest you come to seeing how kids author their own reading lives.

At the very earliest stages, the time children spend reading might look different than it does at later stages. McIntyre et al. (2006) suggest that when children are just beginning to read conventionally, independent reading time will sometimes be more mediated by a teacher. Simply handing a book to a child and sending him off to read isn't necessarily the most powerful way to help that student get better as a reader. Instead, readers benefit from reading aloud with and to each other, engaging in repeated reading, partner reading, choral reading, and echo reading of a book, and doing this in a structured environment that supports the development of the child.

Teachers who are new to the reading workshop model, or new to designating some time specifically for independent reading, are sometimes worried about management, and rightly so. Management matters, because in a well-managed classroom, youngsters are able to read with more stamina. One way to support classroom management and stamina is by asking readers to find a private reading place for themselves. Those who do not have difficulty staying engaged with a book are then encouraged to find a place in the classroom where they can do their best work as a reader. Eventually half the class may be reading at their desks (with empty seats beside them, which allows us to pull in easily to confer), while others each have a long-term "reading nook." With students spread across the classroom, it is easy for you to move from student to student or group to group for instruction.

However, when some students have reading spots around the room, while others continue to read at their desks, your children will need a way to get your attention—a way that you have approved! Otherwise, when they feel stuck and need you or your designee, they grow restless. You'll probably want a standing policy that anyone who really needs you should follow you around as you confer with another student.

Many teachers find it helpful to provide each student with a "book baggie" or "book bin." When children go to the classroom or school library and choose books, they put those books in their personal baggie or bin. This way, readers have a bunch of books "on deck," so when they finish one book, they immediately begin the next, without roaming around the classroom. This process of planned book selection supports engagement in sustained reading.

If your reading time begins with a minilesson or a read-aloud, afterward children can head off to read, carrying their books and their reading tools, such as Post-its. Experts recommend that children read for half an hour in school and an equal length of time at home. If a student can read a level C book in just a few minutes, she could get through ten or more books in thirty minutes. At reading level M, children should be able to read 100–200 words per minute, so on average children could read one of the Magic Tree House books in school each day and an another at home that night.

If a child is struggling to stay engaged in her books, chances are good that she is holding books she can't actually read. Sit alongside that child and ask, "Where are you in the book?" and once the child has told you where he or she is, ask for a summary. "I haven't read that book. Can you tell me what's happening?" Listen with rapt attention and try hard to grasp the story from what the child says, asking a few questions so that you can follow her rendition. If you can't piece together the story's logic, say something like, "It seems a little confusing. Is this book a confusing one?" You really mean, "Is this book too hard for you?" but the child generally will find is easier to disparage the book. "Yeah," she'll say. "It is a *really* confusing book." Then you have a pretty good indication that the book is too hard.

You will also want the child to read aloud to you. Just listen for intonation that shows the child understands what he or she is reading. It will be totally clear from the intonation alone. Does the child's reading sound like talk? Do the sentences sound sensible? Meanwhile, quickly count miscues. Is the child reading with 96% accuracy, at least? If not, the book is probably too hard, and you will want to match that child to a book that is within reach. For more help with that, see the assessment section of Chapter 6, "Assessing Students and Matching Readers to Books."

4 Conferring and Small-Group Work

Helping to Lift the Level of Your Students' Reading through Conferring

Denny Taylor once said, "There is never a time when I pull my chair alongside a child and a miracle doesn't appear." When you draw your chair alongside a child to observe as he reads, you can, with a glance, see if today's book is representative of what that child has been reading. Does this reader seem to choose light, humorous books consistently? Might you want to nudge him to widen his repertoire?

You'll want to carefully observe your students as they read, and do this often. Many years ago, Ken Goodman taught teachers to watch children as they read, attending closely to any departures—or *miscues*—from the text and using this data as a goldmine (Goodman 1965). These errors are not random and each is partially right, so each miscue provides a window into a learner's mental process and helps you detect patterns of errors that can inform your teaching.

One major way you will want to lift the level of your students' reading work is by meeting with them regularly to discuss their thinking process as they read. It can be helpful to classify reading conferences. You might confer with a reader following the *research-decide-teach* structure integral to your writing conferences. You can also *coach* into a child's reading, and you can be a *partner* to a child who is reading. Often you will do a combination of these three things.

Typically, you will want to sit close to your student and observe his external reading behaviors. With your level E reader, you might be noticing if he is still pointing to each word as he tracks print across the page. With a level K reader, you might notice if he is silently engaging with his book, eyes sweeping down the page taking in the story. After a moment or two, you will want to stop your reader, asking, "Can I interrupt you for a minute?" You will then want to jump into a quick conversation about his reading work. You might ask, "Can you read to me for a bit?" or you might ask, "What are you working on today as a reader? Can you show me where you tried that?" Another option might be to follow up on an earlier conversation: "Last time we met, you were working on your fluency. How's that going?"

After you have gotten a quick snapshot of what your reader is thinking and doing in his book, you will want to choose one thing to work on with your reader to quickly help lift the level of his reading. Once you have given your reader a tip, you will want to take a few minutes to teach your reader how using this new information will look in his own reading. You might choose to demonstrate the work, asking the reader to "be like a detective and study the work I do when I read," or you might say, "Let's try this together, then you can try on your own." After you have given some instruction, you will want the reader to try out his new strategy. As he works, you might jump in with short prompts: "Don't forget to . . ." or "Try that again." As you wrap up your conference, you will want to remind your reader that the strategy extends beyond his current book and the current day. You might say, "Remember, whenever you are reading from now on, you will . . ."

After the conference you will want to create a record so that both you and the reader realize you have now come to an agreement. At the end of the conference, you might say to the child, "So tell me what you are going to do," and then at least one of you should write down the plan. You might note in on the child's reading log or in a record book. What matters is that this record informs the reader as he or she continues to work, and informs your next conference.

Helping to Lift the Level of Your Students' Reading through Small-Group Work

The first and most important thing to say about small-group work is this: Do it! The good news is that while your kids are reading up a storm, reaping the bounties of your Classroom Library, you can easily pull together several small groups each day. You need to make leading a small group into no big deal.

GUIDELINES TO INFORM YOUR SMALL-GROUP WORK
Here are a few tips that can generally help all of your small-group work:

- Choose what and how to teach. Don't try to teach the text, but instead, teach the reader something he or she could use another day, with another text. That is, teach a transferable skill or strategy.

- Keep your teaching short. Imagine that in a ten-minute small group, you are talking and demonstrating no more than two minutes. Remember, the person doing the most work is the person who is learning the most.

- To effectively demonstrate, name the teaching point ("One thing I want to teach you is that readers find that when they want to . . . it often helps to . . ."). Then show them how to do this, probably by returning to a part of a familiar class read-aloud.

- Coach kids to try doing the new work themselves, perhaps leaving them with a scaffold like a short list of sentence starters or a chart of steps to follow.

- Let kids know you will check in again soon, and when you do so, follow up, reminding them to add what you have taught to their repertoire of strategies.

Small-group work will be more powerful if you do smaller bouts of it across time than if you have one gigantic small-group session every few weeks. It helps to work with a particular small group for around ten minutes, two or three times a week, for a week or two, rather than working with that group once every week or two, each time for half an hour. The advantage of more frequent short meetings is that you can channel children to do some work related to the group between your meetings. This allows the group work to influence children's reading for broader stretches of time.

THERE IS NO *ONE* WAY TO LEAD SMALL GROUPS. THE BEST IS TO
DRAW FROM A REPERTOIRE OF POSSIBLE SMALL GROUPS.

We encourage you to develop a repertoire of ways of working with small groups.
Native Alaskans, lore has it, have twenty-six words for *snow*. They're such experts
on snow that they don't think of all that white stuff as just one monolithic thing.
With increasing expertise, you can also realize that all your small-group work
does not need to fit into one template or bear a single label. On the contrary, for
your small-group teaching to be responsive, you need to outgrow any feeling that
every small group proceeds in the same way. You might have been trained that you
begin every small group by distributing copies of the same text to a small group
of matched readers, then giving a text introduction, followed by a time in which
readers each read that text while you circle among them, listening to one child and
then another read aloud while you coach into each individual's reading. Yes, that
is one way that small groups can go. Many people refer to that format as guided
reading.

But know that other teachers do entirely different things under the name of
guided reading; it is a term that has vastly different interpretations in one school
and another. In some communities, guided reading entails children gathering, carrying whatever book they are in the midst of reading, and the teacher then talks
a bit about a strategy—perhaps, for example, the teacher points out that some
dialogue is untagged and shows kids that when the text doesn't say who is talking,
the reader mentally adds that information in, keeping track always of who is talking. Then the teacher channels the group members to continue reading wherever
they left off in their book, and the teacher circulates among the group members,
asking each to read aloud a bit when the teacher is there, with the teacher coaching into that reading.

This underscores the point that there is no single way to lead guided reading
groups or to lead small groups. You have choices. One thing we know for certain
about young readers is they are not all the same! At a conference at Teachers College, the reading researcher Richard Allington recently reported that most teachers
have only one format for their small groups. The irony is that we work with small
groups instead of the whole class pre-
cisely so that we can tailor our teaching
to our students.

When you work with small groups,
you can work in out-of-the-box ways,
trying something bold that you have
never tried before, just on the off-chance
it might help. After all, your small-group
instruction will be your forum for working with students for whom in-the-box
sorts of teaching may not have done the
job. For example, think about all the ways
in which you teach reading to your whole
class. Consider whether each of those
ways of teaching reading might be done
in small groups. Presumably you read

aloud to your whole class and engage kids in accountable talk conversations. Why not lead small groups that help kids needing extra support learning how to participate well in that work? You probably engage the whole class in shared reading, orchestrating the class to read a text aloud chorally, in unison. Wouldn't some students benefit from small-group shared reading? Then, too, might you engage small groups of students in word study?

My point is that I think it is helpful for you to imagine a wide repertoire of sorts of small groups.

Planning a Sequence of Small Groups

Imagine small groups as occurring across a sequence of days, building off each other, with you deliberately removing some of the scaffolds as the group becomes more practiced.

For example, you might plan a sequence of small groups to support kids reading texts that are a bit harder than those they have been reading on their own. For your first session, you may tell readers that you believe they are ready to handle texts that are a notch harder than those they have been reading, and you may then give a text introduction to what they will be reading in sync with each other. In your text introduction, instead of simply telling them about the book they'll read, you will want to do so in ways that show them how to orient themselves to future books. So you'll say, "Let's preview this book, as readers do, to get ready to read." Then you might say, "I usually look first to see if there are headings and introductory comments, don't you? Let's look." In that way, you walk kids through the sources of whatever orienting comments you will give them. You might then say, "The other thing I do before I read is think about some of the challenging words I'm apt to encounter," and you could show kids how you skim for those words, and that would then set you up to explain a few. Your introduction will provide more information than kids could have extrapolated themselves, but my point is you do this work in a way that sets kids up to do it themselves. You will probably also want to let readers know about a way in which the texts they are reading these days will pose challenges, and help them with one or two of those challenges. Then kids can get started reading, while you either listen to one child after another and coach into their reading, or while you check the rest of the class.

The next day, when you reconvene this group, you will not want to provide as much scaffolding. You might ask kids to preview the text themselves, constructing their own approximation of a text introduction, with you chiming in to coach or to help as needed. By the third session, you might set readers up to work individually, on their own, and then to teach each other what they noticed, with you again coaching in. In that way, you go from heavily supported guided reading to more lightly supported.

As you plan your small groups, anticipate using the gradual release of responsibility model to progress from heavy to light scaffolding as learners become more proficient in the strategy you are teaching. The concept of scaffolded instruction was first used by Wood et al. (1976) to talk about children's language development. Referring to the temporary structures that are installed and eventually removed from around a building under construction, they suggested that by varying the amounts of scaffolding, learners could be successful. This is an important principle of teaching. Teachers provide learners with maximum support for something that is just beyond their reach, and then gradually remove that support so learners can function with increasing autonomy (Pearson and Gallagher 1983).

Approach any small-group work as an ongoing research project. You are continually researching the children, their needs, and their response to your instruction. Bringing a research stance and a sense of innovation to your small groups will ensure they are joyful, energetic parts of your children's reading lives and your teaching days.

⑤ Partnerships

The books that matter in our lives are the books we have discussed. "It takes two to read a book," Alan Purves has said, and it is often true in our lives that the books we remember most are those we have shared.

Lev Vygotsky has helped us realize that by encouraging students to interact with others, we give them frames for thinking alone. If students repeatedly say to each other, "So what do you think this is really about?" they will soon ask that question of themselves. The conversations that our students have "in the air" will become conversations they have in their own minds.

Readers need to read and talk back to books in the social world of the classroom for both interpersonal and intellectual reasons. When you teach comprehension, much of what you teach is depth of listening, understanding, and response. Part of teaching comprehension, then, is making a place for astute and active listening. If you want children to listen to an author, won't you also want children to listen to each other, to link their ideas with those of their classmates? If you want children to empathize with characters in books, won't you want them to hear each other's ideas and perspectives and see these worlds and texts through each other's eyes?

The books that matter in our lives are the books we have discussed.

In many classrooms, each child is partnered with another child, and those partnerships are matched-level partnerships because the readers often read the same books—sometimes in sync with each other and more often in sequence, with one reading a book first, then the other reading it. In a swap-book partnership, for example, both readers could be reading two books from the Katie Woo series, with one reading *Katie Woo Has the Flu* and another reading *Katie and the Fancy Substitute*. Then, they can swap when they're finished. This ensures that at least half the time, children will be talking about books that their partner knows well, and regardless they are sharing in books with the same characters and overall plot structure. If one reader is ready to proceed to more challenging texts before the other partner is, you may need to finesse this by creating temporary triads. There is another reason for triads—for English language learners, the partnerships or triads often contain a more and less proficient speaker of English. For new arrivals, the partnerships may be language based, for example, two speakers of Urdu working together.

Once you have your students matched in reading partnerships and reading books, you'll want to consider the times in which they can work with their partners. Many teachers choose to have students sit with their partners on the rug or at their tables during reading workshop, and they'll regularly ask students to turn and talk with their partner across the minilesson, saying things like "Partner 1, can you tell Partner 2 what you're noticing about the characters in your reading today?" Partners might work together for a few minutes during the mid-workshop teaching that comes midway through the lesson. Then, the workshop might end with five minutes of time for partner conversations.

There's a variety of work that partners can do as they work together. Your youngest readers will spend significant time simply reading their books together as partners, helping each other practice their word-solving strategies and building reading fluency. They may read chorally, or they may take turns, with one reading one page and the other, the next page, or they may echo read, with one reading the book straight through, then the other doing so. Partners will also talk about their books, and you can teach kids the kinds of talk that partners do. Let them know that partners sometimes recall a book, retelling it to each other. They sometimes reflect on favorite pages, rereading those pages and talking about why they are special, and how those pages connect to the whole book. They ask questions, and think together about those questions. They talk about ways a book reminds them of another book, or of real life.

If you would like to see videos of partnerships in action, visit the Teachers College Reading and Writing Project's Vimeo site at www.vimeo.com/tcrwp. A particular favorite video shows a fourth-grade partnership discussing *Old Yeller* (https://vimeo.com/55954403). Although the students are older than yours, there is much to learn from their work together. Watch this video and take note of the moves the partners make. Notice how the students move beyond retelling what happened in the text, engaging each other by zooming in on powerful parts in the book, acting out those parts, and discussing their significance. As your students begin tackling more and more complex texts, this is the work you will want them to engage in.

To Support Your Students' Reading Lives, Energize Your Own Reading

In the end, the best thing you can do to nourish and energize your students' independent reading lives is to nourish and energize your own. We all need to make the time to burrow under the covers and read that tantalizing book, to read the newspaper, to track down the picture book we adored when we were six, to order the new Pulitzer Prize winner or the latest beach book. We need to be adult readers, and we need to know the books in our Classroom Libraries, too. Having read these books, you can authentically pull alongside a child to say, "Did you just finish the latest Judy Moody book? Can you believe that . . . ?!" We need to do this, because by reading we layer our experience and develop greater breadth and depth to draw on in our teaching. But we need to do this most of all, because when we love reading, when we ourselves draw power and strength and peace from reading, we educate our students' imagination about what their own world of reading can be.